The COMMODORE 64 Experience

The COMMODORE 64 Experience

By
Mike Dean Klein

Edited by
William B. Sanders, Ph.D.

Illustrations by
Tes Bonnarith

DATAMOST INC

8943 Fullbright Ave., Chatsworth, CA 91311-2750
(818) 709-1202

DATAMOST™

ISBN 0-88190-230-6

ACKNOWLEDGEMENTS

I would like to thank a few people who helped me with the production of this book. One is Bill Sanders, author of *THE ELEMENTARY COMMODORE 64*. I wouldn't have done the book had it not been for his trust in me. Thanks to Bill and DATAMOST for the opportunity. I would like to send a BIG thank you to Roger Wagner of Southwestern Data Systems for letting me use their Commodore 64 assembler **MERLIN.** Without it, I would have been working at a much slower pace. Its performance is unbelievable. (A definite must for the serious machine language programmer.) Another thanks to Skyles Electric Works, for putting out the VIC-tree, a 'cartridge' which adds many new BASIC commands. A programmers delight!

Thanks to my girlfriend Patty Pollmann, for being understanding about my lack of time. I'll make a programmer out of her yet! Lastly, thanks to my close friends, for all their encouragement and support:

Kevin Kelly
Bill Parker
June Klein
David Klein
Don Klein
Joel Johnstone
Dean Garrett
Doug Sherburne
Mark Berry

EDITOR'S INTRODUCTION

William B. Sanders, Ph.D.

How many times have you heard someone say, "But what can you *do* with your computer?" This is an important question for both new owners of computers and those who are considering the purchase of their first home computer. For those who have a COMMODORE 64, that question is not limited by the number of things one can do; but rather by the exhaustive list of applications!

There are two ways to make your computer operate. One is to buy programs and run them on your computer. Just let them do their magic, sit back, and watch. A second is to learn how to program and write your own software. The first method can be expensive, but you have programs that do everything from word processing to playing games. The second method can be a lot of fun, but it takes time for you to be able to program your computer to do what you want.

This book represents a third alternative. It helps you learn how to write programs and at the same time gives you programs you can use right away. If you are not interested in learning how to program, just key in the listings as they appear in this book and save them to tape tape or disk. When you want to use them, just LOAD and RUN them, and they will happily perform. On the other hand, if you want to learn how to program at the same time you are copying in application programs, this book will show you many programmer's tricks. The best way to learn something is to be shown a useful application, and the programs in this book do just that.

The COMMODORE 64 EXPERIENCE was designed to provide a wide range of applications to be of use to everyone. It is arranged into five distinct sections:

I HOME
II EDUCATION
III ENTERTAINMENT
IV BUSINESS
V UTILITY PROGRAMS

The first part is a collection of programs that have a wide variety of applications in the home. Domestic chores, such as cooking, are made simpler with a Recipe Book program that will give you immediate access to your favorite recipe. (It won't fix dinner . . . yet.) For EDUCATIONAL applications, you will find several programs to help children learn everything from their Math to the Capitals of the various states. Third, the ENTERTAINMENT section has a number of games you can play with your computer as well as a drawing program to create designs and pictures in high resolution graphics. For the business person, there are several programs to aid in decision making and financial planning. If you would like to see stock market graphs, the Business Graph program will make annual graphs for you. Finally, for the programmer, there are several UTILITY programs. "Utilities" are programs that help you program. You like sprites, but it's more trouble than it's worth to make them? The Sprite Creator will give you all the information you need and help you build them. Several other utilities will help the programmer both in writing programs and understanding how to program.

As you can see, the *COMMODORE 64 EXPERIENCE* has a wide variety of computer applications. What's more, you can modify the programs to your own particular needs and tastes. All of the programs are clearly presented and explained, and while they will work perfectly well as they are presented, there is no mystery if you want to change them.

The author of the *COMMODORE 64 EXPERIENCE,* Mike Klein, is a seasoned programmer, not only on the COMMODORE 64 but on other microcomputers as well. However, the features of the COMMODORE 64 allowed Mike to use a wide variety of programming applications not readily available on other microcomputers—such as sprite graphics. With an eye on both clarity and practicality, Mike created this collection of programs so that they could be used and understood by both the novice and experienced programmer.

TABLE OF CONTENTS

Section 1

Programs for the Home

- Recipe Book
- Shopping List
- Phone Book
- Kitchen Metrics
- Budget Helper

PROGRAMS FOR THE HOME

There are many uses for a home computer in the home. Obviously, it is possible to use several of the programs under EDUCATION, ENTERTAINMENT and BUSINESS in the home, but in designing programs for the home, I was somewhat stumped. After all, what exactly is 'the home?' Does it mean entertainment for the kids or help for the housewife? Or does it signify business programs for the fathers and mothers? Well, the first and the last are already covered in the book, so I chose to help the person in between. The programs I thought would be most useful around the house are a Phone Book with a search capability, (also a handy program for your business), a Recipe Book (to keep track of recipe data), and a Shopping List program (prints out a weekly shopping list when items are entered into it). Finally, Kitchen Metrics is provided for figuring out metric notations, and Budget Helper will assist your children in keeping tabs on their allowance.

Recipe Book

I'm not sure why, but one of the programs I enjoyed writing the most was the Recipe Book program. Maybe it's the fact that it did a lot and was easy to write. One gets a certain amount of pride from a program that works correctly and that performs a particular task. With Recipe Book, you have the ability to write a recipe to disk and call it back at will. There are five basic commands in the menu:

1) Enter file name:
2) Edit/examine ingredients
3) Write recipe
4) Read recipe
5) Quit

The only selection that needs explaining is number 2. Enter a 2 to bring you up to the second menu:

1) List ingredients
2) Delete ingredients
3) Add ingredients
4) Return to main menu

Now, enter a 1 to give a list of all the ingredients that you have entered so far. If you wish to delete a particular ingredient, remember it's number in the list, and type a 2. Then enter the number of the item that you wish to delete. Upon listing the ingredients again, you will find that it is gone from your list. Adding ingredients is done by entering a 3. Ingredients are entered one at a time, each one separated by a carriage return. When you have finished, simply enter a carriage return with nothing behind it. Entering a 4 will bring you back to the original menu. Remember that you must enter a file name before you can read or write anything on the disk!

```
10 REM ******************
20 REM *** INITIALIZE ***
30 REM ******************
40 PRINT CHR$(147)CHR$(144)
50 POKE 53280,1 : POKE 53281,1
60 DIM INGR$(30) : FILE$=""
70 REM *************************
80 REM *** PROGRAM START ***
90 REM *************************
100 F$="": GOSUB 1270
110 PRINT CHR$(19) : PRINT : PRINT
120 PRINT "CHOOSE ONE:" : PRINT
130 PRINT "<1> RECIPE FILE NAME:";
140 PRINT CHR$(18)FILE$CHR$(146)
150 PRINT "<2> EDIT/EXAM. INGREDIENTS"
160 PRINT "<3> WRITE RECIPE TO DISK"
170 PRINT "<4> READ RECIPE FROM DISK"
180 PRINT "<5> QUIT"
```

```
190 PRINT CHR$(19) : PRINT : PRINT
200 FOR T=1 TO 11
210 PRINT CHR$(29);
220 NEXT
230 INPUT F$
240 F= VAL (F$)
250 IF F<1 OR F>5 THEN 100
260 ON F GOTO 310,430,1020,1130
270 PRINT CHR$(147)"BYE BYE. . ." : END
280 REM ***************************
290 REM *** ENTER FILE NAME ***
300 REM ***************************
310 GOSUB 1270
320 FILE$=""
330 PRINT CHR$(19) : PRINT : PRINT
340 PRINT : PRINT
350 PRINT "RECIPE FILE NAME:";
360 INPUT FILE$
370 IF FILE$="" THEN 100
380 IF LEN (FILE$)>16 THEN 310
390 GOTO 100
400 REM ****************************
410 REM *** ENTER DATA MODE ***
420 REM ****************************
430 F$="" : GOSUB 1270
440 PRINT CHR$(19) : PRINT : PRINT
450 PRINT "MENU:" : PRINT
460 PRINT "<1> LIST INGREDIENTS"
470 PRINT "<2> DELETE INGREDIENTS"
480 PRINT "<3> ADD INGREDIENTS"
490 PRINT "<4> RETURN TO MENU"
500 PRINT CHR$(19) :PRINT : PRINT
510 FOR T=1TO 5:PRINT CHR$(29); : NEXT
520 INPUT F$
530 F= VAL (F$)
540 IF F<1OR F>4 THEN 430
550 ON F GOTO 590,750,900,100
```

```
560 REM ****************************
570 REM *** LIST INGREDIENTS ***
580 REM ****************************
590 GOSUB 1270
600 PRINT CHR$(19) : PRINT : PRINT
610 FORT=1 TO INGR
620 PRINT "#";T;" ";INGR$(T)
630 IF T=19 THEN 680
640 NEXT
650 PRINT "THAT'S IT"
660 GOSUB 1380
670 GOTO 430
680 PRINT "PRESS A KEY"
690 GOSUB 1380 : GOSUB 1270
700 PRINT CHR$(19) : PRINT : PRINT
710 GOTO 640
720 REM *******************************
730 REM *** DELETE INGREDIENTS ***
740 REM *******************************
750 GOSUB 1270 : F$=""
760 PRINT CHR$(19) : PRINT : PRINT
770 PRINT "WHICH # TO DELETE:";
780 INPUT F$
790 IF F$="" THEN 430
800 NUM= VAL (F$)
810 IF NUM<1 OR NUM>INGR THEN 430
820 FOR T=NUM TO INGR-1
830 INGR$(T)=INGR$(T+1)
840 NEXT
850 INGR=INGR-1
860 GOTO 430
870 REM ****************************
880 REM *** ADD INGREDIENTS ***
890 REM ****************************
900 GOSUB 1270
910 PRINT CHR$(19) : PRINT : PRINT
920 PRINT "INGREDIENT#";INGR+1;":";
930 INGR$=""
```

```
940 INPUT INGR$
950 IF INGR$="" THEN 430
960 INGR=INGR+1
970 INGR$(INGR)=INGR$
980 GOTO 920
990 REM   ****************************
1000 REM *** WRITE OUT RECIPE ***
1010 REM ****************************
1020 IF FILE$="" THEN 100
1030 GOSUB 1270
1040 PRINT "WRITING OUT RECIPE DATA"
1050 OPEN 9,8,9,"0:"+FILE$+",S,W"
1060 FOR T=1 TO INGR
1070 PRINT#9,INGR$(T)
1080 NEXT
1090 CLOSE 9 : GOTO 100
1100 REM ************************
1110 REM *** READ IN RECIPE ***
1120 REM ************************
1130 IF FILE$="" THEN 100
1140 GOSUB 1270
1150 PRINT CHR$(19) :PRINT : PRINT
1160 PRINT
1170 PRINT "READING IN RECIPE DATA"
1180 OPEN 9,8,9,"0:"+FILE$+",S,R"
1190 INGR=0
1200 INGR=INGR+1
1210 INPUT#9,INGR$(INGR)
1220 IF ST=0 THEN 1200
1230 CLOSE 9 : GOTO 100
1240 REM ****************************
1250 REM *** PRINT TOP BORDER ***
1260 REM ****************************
1270 PRINT CHR$(147)TAB(14);
1280 PRINT "RECIPE BOOK"
1290 PRINT TAB(14);
1300 FOR T=1 TO 11
1310 PRINT CHR$(163);
```

```
1320 NEXT
1330 PRINT
1340 RETURN
1350 REM  *****************
1360 REM *** GET KEY ***
1370 REM  *****************
1380 GETR$ : IF R$="" THEN 1380
1390 RETURN
```

Shopping List

How many shopping lists look more like shredded beef than paper? All those nasty erasures and scribbles! With Shopping List, you can proofread your grocery items before they are printed out to your printer or to the screen. You can add and delete items from your list at will, by entering 1 and 2 respectively. The number of items it will hold is up to you. All you have to do is change the DIM statement at the beginning of the program to reflect the number of items you wish the list to contain. The entire list may be dumped to either the screen or the printer by selecting option 3 from the main menu. If you press 3 the program will ask you whether you want it on the <S>creen or the <P>rinter. Enter an S or a P depending on which you prefer. It's as easy as that! With your shopping list, you will be sure that you can read everything you have included and save an extra trip to the market.

```
10 DIM ITEMS$(50): ITEM=0
20 REM *********************
30 REM *** SET SCREEN ***
40 REM *********************
50 PRINT CHR$(147)CHR$(144)
60 POKE 53280,1
70 POKE 53281,1
80 REM ************************
90 REM *** PRINT SCREEN ***
100 REM ************************
110 GOSUB 300
120 PRINT CHR$(19) : PRINT
130 PRINT : PRINT
140 PRINT "MENU:"
150 PRINT
160 PRINT "<1> ADD TO SHOPPING LIST"
170 PRINT "<2> DELETE FROM LIST"
180 PRINT "<3> DUMP LIST"
190 PRINT "<4> QUIT"
200 GET A$ : IF A$="" THEN 200
210 A= VAL (A$)
```

```
220 IF A<1 OR A>4 THEN 300
230 ON A GOTO 350,460,610
240 PRINT CHR$(147)"BYE BYE. . . ."
250 PRINT : PRINT : PRINT
260 END
270 REM ******************************
280 REM *** PRINT TOP BORDER ***
290 REM ******************************
300 PRINT CHR$(147)TAB(16)"GROCERIES"
310 PRINT TAB(16)"---------" : RETURN
320 REM **********************************
330 REM *** ADD TO SHOPPING LIST ***
340 REM **********************************
350 GOSUB 300
360 PRINT CHR$(19) : PRINT : PRINT
370 PRINT "ITEM#";ITEM+1;":";
380 ITEM$(ITEM)=""
390 INPUT ITEM$(ITEM)
400 IF ITEM$(ITEM)="" THEN 110
410 ITEM=ITEM+1
420 GOTO 370
430 REM ************************************
440 REM *** DELETE ITEMS FROM LIST ***
450 REM ************************************
460 GOSUB 300
470 PRINT CHR$(19) : PRINT : PRINT
480 A$=""
490 INPUT "DELETE WHICH ITEM#:";A$
500 IF A$="" THEN 110
510 A= VAL (A$)
520 IF A<0 OR A>ITEM THEN 110
530 FOR T=A-1 TO ITEM-1
540 ITEM$(T)=ITEM$(T+1)
550 NEXT
560 ITEM=ITEM-1
570 GOTO 110
580 REM ********************************
590 REM *** DUMP SHOPPING LIST ***
600 REM ********************************
```

```
610 GOSUB 300
620 PRINT CHR$(19) : PRINT : PRINT
630 A$=""
640 PRINT "<P>RINTER OR <S>CREEN:"
650 GET A$ : IF A$="" THEN 650
660 IF A$<>"P" AND A$<>"S" THEN 110
670 IF A$="S" THEN 810
680 REM *********************************
690 REM *** DUMP LIST TO PRINTER ***
700 REM *********************************
710 OPEN 1,5
720 PRINT#1,"GROCERY LIST"
730 PRINT#1,CHR$(13),CHR$(13)
740 FOR T=0 TO ITEM-1
750 PRINT#1,ITEM$(T)
760 NEXT : CLOSE 1
770 GOTO 110
780 REM *********************************
790 REM *** DUMP LIST TO SCREEN ***
800 REM *********************************
810 GOSUB 300
820 PRINT CHR$(19) : PRINT : PRINT
830 IF ITEM=0 THEN 940
840 FOR T=0 TO ITEM-1
850 PRINT "ITEM#";T+1;":";ITEM$(T)
860 NEXT
870 PRINT
880 PRINT "HIT RETURN TO RESUME"
890 GET R$ : IF R$<>CHR$(13) THEN 890
900 GOTO 110
910 REM *********************************
920 REM *** NO ITEMS ENTERED YET ***
930 REM *********************************
940 PRINT
950 PRINT "NO ITEMS HAVE BEEN ENTERED!"
960 GET R$ : IFR$="" THEN 960
970 GOTO 110
```

Phone Book

Phone Book is the largest program in this book, as well it should be! It is capable of a wide variety of functions. It is my personal favorite, because I use it more than any other program. With it, you can enter names and numbers (the computer inserts them into the file alphabetically), search and recall them, print all of the entries delete them, and get printouts of the entire proceedings. Here is the menu you should see, upon completion of entering the program:

<1> ENTER NAME AND NUMBER
<2> SEARCH FOR ENTRY
<3> DELETE ENTRY
<4> DUMP ALL ENTRIES
<5> INIT PHONE FILE
<6> QUIT

The last option is probably self-explanatory, but the others need some explaining. When the program is first RUN, you should initialize a Phone Directory File, by typing a 5. It will then ask you if you are sure. Enter a Y if you are, or an N if you aren't. You should only initialize a file once, as any subsequent attempt to do so will erase all the old information that is in that file. You do not want that to happen. Once you have initialized the file you may start entering your information, via number 1. Typing in a 1 will display the following questions:

LAST NAME:
FIRST NAME:
AREA CODE:619
PHONE#:

(In case you are wondering why there are no question marks with the INPUT statements, it's because I opened a file to the screen, and that eliminates the little buggers.) Notice that there is a 619 after the area code. Merely by pressing RETURN, that AREA CODE will be entered. You may want to change it to an area code that you use frequently (in line 410). When all the questions have been answered, you will be asked:

ARE THEY RIGHT (Y/N/X):X

Respond with a Y for YES, an N for NO, and an X for exit. Again, hitting a RETURN immediately will put you back into the MAIN MENU. If you answer a Y for YES the drive will whirr for a bit (be patient, it's sorting!), and then, TAH DAH! an entry has been made.

Option 2 on the main menu is the SEARCH and RECALL ROUTINE. By typing in a 2, you will get the following screen display:

WHICH:
<1> LAST NAME
<2> FIRST NAME
<3> AREA CODE
<4> PHONE #
<5> QUIT

Let's pick a person for our example, and use the name PATTY POLLMANN. If you wanted to search for the first name, PATTY, because you forgot her last name, then enter a 2. Now it will ask you which item it should search for. Enter PATTY. The drive will whirr for a bit, and all of the PATTYs you have entered, will be listed up on the screen. The same procedure applies to items 1, 3, and 4. Entering a 5 will put you back in the MAIN MENU. Whoops! What if you suddenly realize that you have entered PATTY's phone number incorrectly? Don't worry. All you have to do is re-enter all her data again. First delete the original entry by typing a 3 from the MAIN MENU. The computer will ask you for the same information it did in the SEARCH AND RECALL process. Since you know there is only one POLLMANN in the entire directory, enter a 1 for last name. Now enter "POLLMANN", and the computer will go through and delete all the POLLMANNs on disk. Finally, choose option 1 from the MAIN MENU to re-enter all her data again.

Suppose you have Patty's, and several others' entries right this time, and you want to view them all. This can be accomplished by entering a 4. The computer will dump every name and number it has in its file onto the screen. *When you are in the SEARCH or DUMP mode, you can temporarily halt the printing of entries by pressing the* SPACE BAR. Pressing it again will continue the listing, but pressing any other key will return you to the MAIN MENU. Also, when you enter either of these modes, it will ask you if you want it to print the entries on the printer or list them on the screen. Enter a P or an S. Notice that if you select the printer, the entries will be displayed on the screen as well. Here's a complete listing of the program:

```
10 REM ********************
20 REM *** SET SCREEN ***
30 REM ********************
40 PRINT CHR$(147)CHR$(144)
50 PRINT CHR$(142)CHR$(8)
60 OPEN 1,0
70 C$=CHR$(13)
80 BK$=CHR$(157)
90 POKE 53280,1 : POKE 53281,1
100 REM **********************
110 REM *** PRINT SCREEN ***
120 REM **********************
130 PRINT CHR$(147)TAB(15)"PHONE BOOK"
140 PRINT : PRINT : PRINT
150 PRINT "MENU:" : PRINT
160 PRINT "<1> ENTER NAME & NUMBER"
170 PRINT "<2> SEARCH FOR ENTRY"
180 PRINT "<3> DELETE ENTRY"
190 PRINT "<4> DUMP ALL ENTRIES"
200 PRINT "<5> INITIALIZE PHONE FILE"
210 PRINT "<6> QUIT"
220 PRINT CHR$(19) : PRINT : PRINT
230 PRINT : PRINT TAB(5);
240 POKE 198,0
250 INPUT#1,A$
```

```
260 A= VAL (A$)
270 IF A<1 OR A>6 THEN 130
280 ON A GOTO 340,1540,1910,1050,1410
290 PRINT CHR$(147)CHR$(9)"BYE BYE"
300 PRINT : PRINT : CLOSE 1 : END
310 REM *********************************
320 REM *** ENTER NAME & NUMBER ***
330 REM *********************************
340 PRINT CHR$(147)
350 PRINT "LAST NAME:";
360 INPUT#1,LN$
370 PRINT
380 PRINT "FIRST NAME:";
390 INPUT#1,FI$
400 PRINT
410 PRINT "AREA CODE:619"BK$BK$BK$;
420 INPUT#1,AC$
430 PRINT
440 PRINT "PHONE#:";
450 INPUT#1,PN$
460 PRINT
470 PRINT : PRINT
480 PRINT "ARE THEY RIGHT (Y/N/X):X"BK$;
490 INPUT#1,A$
500 IF A$="Y" THEN 560
510 IF A$="N" THEN 340
520 GOTO 130
530 REM ************************
540 REM *** TRANSFER DATA ***
550 REM ************************
560 OPEN 4,8,4,"0:PHONE FILE.DATA,S,R"
570 OPEN 5,8,5,"0:COPY,S,W"
580 INPUT#4,A$(1),A$(2),A$(3),A$(4)
590 IF A$(1)="EOF" THEN
PRINT#5,LN$C$FI$C$AC$C$PN$ : GOTO 710
600 IF ASC (A$(1))<ASC(LN$) THEN 640
610 GOSUB 850
620 IF L1>LN THEN 680
```

```
630 IF L1=LN THEN 660
640 PRINT#5,A$(1)C$A$(2)C$A$(3)C$A$(4)
650 GOTO 580
660 GOSUB 950
670 IF F1<FI THEN 640
680 PRINT#5,LN$C$FI$C$AC$C$PN$
690 PRINT#5,A$(1)C$A$(2)C$A$(3)C$A$(4)
700 INPUT#4,A$(1),A$(2),A$(3),A$(4)
710 PRINT#5,A$(1)C$A$(2)C$A$(3)C$A$(4)
720 IF A$(1)<>"EOF" THEN 700
730 CLOSE 4 : CLOSE 5
740 OPEN 15,8,15
750 PRINT#15,"S0:PHONE FILE.DATA"
760 PRINT#15,"R0:PHONE FILE.DATA=COPY"
770 CLOSE 15
780 GOTO 130
790 REM ************************
800 REM *** ALPHABETIZER ***
810 REM ************************
820 REM  ********************
830 REM  *** LAST NAME***
840 REM  ********************
850 S$=LN$
860 IF LEN(A$(1))<LEN(LN$) THEN S$=A$(1)
870 FOR T=1 TO LEN(S$)
880 L1=ASC(MID$(A$(1),T,1))
890 LN=ASC(MID$(LN$,T,1))
900 IF LN=L1 THEN NEXT : RETURN
910 T=50 : NEXT : RETURN
920 REM  ********************
930 REM *** FIRST NAME ***
940 REM  ********************
950 S$=FI$
960 IF LEN(A1$(2))<LEN(FI$) THEN S$=A$(2)
970 FOR T=1 TO LEN(S$)
980 F1=ASC(MID$(A$(2),T,1))
990 FI=ASC(MID$(FI$,T,1))
1000 IF FI=F1 THEN NEXT:RETURN
```

```
1010 T=50 :  NEXT : RETURN
1020 REM *******************
1030 REM *** DUMP FILE ***
1040 REM *******************
1050 PRINT CHR$(147)
1060 GOSUB 2450
1070 IF O$="S" THEN 1140
1080 OPEN 2,4
1090 PRINT#2,C$
1100 FOR T=1 TO 7
1110 PRINT#2," ";
1120 NEXT
1130 PRINT#2,"PHONE BOOK LISITNG"C$C$
1140 ENTRIES=0
1150 OPEN 5,8,5,"0:PHONE FILE.DATA,S,R"
1160 INPUT#5,LN$,FI$,AC$,PN$
1170 IF LN$="EOF" THEN 1310
1180 GET A$
1190 IF A$<>" " THEN 1230
1200 POKE 198,0
1210 GET A$ : IF A$="" THEN 1210
1220 IF A$<>" " THEN CLOSE 5 : CLOSE 2 :
GOTO 130
1230 IF O$="S" THEN 1260
1240 PRINT#2,"NAME : "LN$","FI$
1250 PRINT#2,"PHONE#: ("AC$")"PN$C$
1260 PRINT LN$","FI$
1270 PRINT "("AC$")"PN$
1280 ENTRIES=ENTRIES+1
1290 PRINT
1300 GOTO 1160
1310 CLOSE 5 : CLOSE 2
1320 D$="END OF FILE DATA"
1330 IF ENTRIES=0 THEN D$="FILE IS EMPTY"
1340 PRINT : PRINT D$
1350 PRINT ENTRIES" IN ALL"
1360 IF PEEK (197)=64 THEN 1360
1370 GOTO 130
```

```
1380 REM ********************************
1390 REM *** INITIALIZE PHONE FILE ***
1400 REM ********************************
1410 PRINT CHR$(147)"ARE YOU SURE (Y/
N):N"BK$;
1420 INPUT#1,A$
1430 IF A$<>"Y" THEN 130
1440 OPEN 15,8,15
1450 PRINT#15,"S0:PHONE FILE.DATA"
1460 CLOSE 15
1470 OPEN 5,8,5,"0:PHONE FILE.DATA,S,W"
1480 PRINT#5,"EOF"C$"Z"C$"Z"C$"Z"
1490 CLOSE 5
1500 GOTO 130
1510 REM *****************************
1520 REM *** SEARCH FOR ENTRY ***
1530 REM *****************************
1540 GOSUB 2240
1550 IF ITEM$="EXIT" OR A=5 THEN 130
1560 GOSUB 2450
1570 IF O$="S" THEN 1600
1580 OPEN 2,4
1590 PRINT#2,C$" PHONE NUMBERS"
1600 OPEN 5,8,5,"0:PHONE FILE.DATA,S,R"
1610 FOUND=0
1620 PRINT CHR$(147)
1630 INPUT#5,A$(1),A$(2),A$(3),A$(4)
1640 IF A$(1)="EOF" THEN 1810
1650 IF ITEM$=A$(A) THEN 1670
1660 GOTO 1630
1670 IF O$="S" THEN 1700
1680 PRINT#2,"NAME : "A$(1)","A$(2)
1690 PRINT#2,"PHONE#: ("A$(3)","A$(4)C$
1700 PRINT A$(1)","A$(2)
1710 PRINT "("A$(3)")"A$(4)
1720 PRINT
1730 FOUND=FOUND+1
1740 GET A$ : IF A$ <>" " THEN 1630
```

```
1750 GET A$ : IF A$="" THEN 1750
1760 IF A$<> " " THEN CLOSE 5 : CLOSE 2 :
GOTO 130
1770 GOTO 1630
1780 REM *********************
1790 REM *** END OF FILE ***
1800 REM *********************
1810 CLOSE 5 : CLOSE 2
1820 PRINT : PRINT
1830 PRINT "END OF FILE"
1840 PRINT "YOU HAD"FOUND"THAT MATCHED"
1850 GET#1,A$
1860 IF A$<>" " THEN 1850
1870 GOTO 130
1880 REM ************************
1890 REM *** DELETE ENTRY ***
1900 REM ************************
1910 GOSUB 2240
1920 IF ITEM$="EXIT" OR A=5 THEN 130
1930 PRINT CHR$(147)
1940 C=0
1950 OPEN 4,8,4,"0:PHONE FILE.DATA,S,R"
1960 OPEN 5,8,5,"0:COPY,S,W"
1970 INPUT#4,A$(1),A$(2),A$(3),A$(4)
1980 IF A$(A)=ITEM$ THEN 2020
1990 PRINT#5,A$(1) C$ A$(2) C$ A$(3) C$ A$(4)
C$
2000 IF A$(1)="EOF" THEN 2110
2010 GOTO 1970
2020 C=1
2030 PRINT A$(1)","A$(2)
2040 PRINT "("A$(3)")"A$(4)
2050 PRINT CHR$(18)"DELETED"
2060 PRINT
2070 GOTO 1970
2080 REM *********************
2090 REM *** END OF FILE ***
2100 REM *********************
2110 CLOSE 4 : CLOSE 5
```

```
2120 OPEN 15,8,15
2130 PRINT#15,"S0:PHONE FILE.DATA"
2140 PRINT#15,"R0:PHONE FILE.DATA=COPY"
2150 CLOSE 15
2160 M$="END OF FILE"+C$+"ITEM NOT
FOUND"
2170 IF C=1 THEN M$="FINISHED"
2180 PRINT : PRINT : PRINT M$
2190 GET A$ : IF A$="" THEN 2190
2200 GOTO 130
2210 REM ******************
2220 REM *** GET ITEM ***
2230 REM ******************
2240 PRINT CHR$(147)"WHICH TYPE:5"
2250 PRINT : PRINT
2260 PRINT "<1> LAST NAME"
2270 PRINT "<2> FIRST NAME"
2280 PRINT "<3> AREA CODE"
2290 PRINT "<4> PHONE#"
2300 PRINT "<5> QUIT"
2310 PRINT
2320 PRINT "ENTER <EXIT> TO LEAVE"
2330 PRINT CHR$(19)TAB(11);
2340 INPUT#1,A$
2350 RETURN
2360 A= VAL (A$)
2370 IF A=5 THEN RETURN
2380 IF A<1 OR A>4 THEN 2240
2390 PRINT : PRINT "SEARCH FOR:";
2400 INPUT#1,ITEM$
2410 RETURN
2420 REM ********************************
2430 REM *** PRINTER OR SCREEN ***
2440 REM ********************************
2450 PRINT CHR$(147)"OUTPUT TO <P>RINTER
OR <S>CREEN:S"BK$;
2460 INPUT#1,O$
2470 IF O$ <>"P" AND O$<>"S" THEN 2450
2480 PRINT CHR$(147) : RETURN
```

Kitchen Metrics

Metrics!? Who knows, or even understands metrics. Sure, everyone knows that there are 100 centigrams in a gram, but who knows exactly how heavy 30 centigrams are? Around the kitchen, some means of converting metrics is needed. Voila! Kitchen Metrics is born. Now you too, can convert metrics in the privacy of your own home.

The menu should look like this:

```
Which:
<1> Quarts—Liters
<2> Liters—Quarts
<3> Ounces—Grams
<4> Grams—Ounces
<5> Fahrenheit—Celsius
<6> Celsius—Fahrenheit
```

Simply type in the number of which conversion you would like, followed by a number. Suppose you would like to find out how many liters are in two quarts. Type a 1 to convert from quarts to liters. When it asks for units, type in a 2, for two quarts. Presto! Your two quarts have been converted into metrics.

```
10 REM ********************
20 REM *** SET SCREEN ***
30 REM ********************
40 PRINT CHR$(147)CHR$(144)
50 POKE 53280,1 : POKE 53281,1
60 REM **********************
70 REM *** PRINT SCREEN ***
80 REM **********************
90 PRINT CHR$(147)TAB(12)"KITCHEN METRICS"
100 PRINT : PRINT
110 PRINT "WHICH:"
120 PRINT
130 PRINT "<1> QUARTS—LITERS"
140 PRINT "<2> LITERS—QUARTS"
150 PRINT "<3> OUNCES—GRAMS"
160 PRINT "<4> GRAMS—OUNCES"
170 PRINT "<5> FAHRENHEIT—CELSIUS"
180 PRINT "<6> CELSIUS—FAHRENHEIT"
190 GET R$ : IF R$="" THEN 190
200 R= VAL (R$)
210 IF R<1 OR R>6 THEN 190
220 PRINT : PRINT
230 INPUT "UNIT:";UNIT
240 ON R GOSUB 320,370,420,470,520,570
250 PRINT : PRINT "CONVERTED IT'S:"AM
260 PRINT
270 INPUT "PRESS RETURN TO CONTINUE:";A$
280 GOTO 90
290 REM ************************
300 REM *** QUARTS—LITERS ***
310 REM ************************
320 AM=.95*UNIT
```

```
330 RETURN
340 REM *************************
350 REM *** LITERS—QUARTS ***
360 REM *************************
370 AM=1.06*UNIT
380 RETURN
390 REM ***************************
400 REM *** OUNCES—GRAMS ***
410 REM ***************************
420 AM=28.35*UNIT
430 RETURN
440 REM ***************************
450 REM *** GRAMS—OUNCES ***
460 REM ***************************
470 AM=.035*UNIT
480 RETURN
490 REM *******************************
500 REM *** FAHRENHEIT—CELSIUS ***
510 REM *******************************
520 AM=(UNIT-32)*5/9
530 RETURN
540 REM *******************************
550 REM *** CELSIUS—FAHRENHEIT ***
560 REM *******************************
570 AM=(UNIT*9/5)+32
580 RETURN
```

Budget Helper

I am not good with money. As soon as I get it, it is as good as gone. You may be that way too. That's why I made Budget Helper. It is designed primarily for younger children to help them budget their allowances. Key a 1 to enter your allowance. Then enter a number from 2–15. You will be prompted for a string and an amount. Simply enter in your expense, such as 'gas for car,' then enter in an amount like 35. Now your current amount of allowance left to spend is shown on the screen, and you are ready to enter more expenses.

```
10 REM ********************
20 REM *** SET SCREEN***
30 REM ********************
40 PRINT CHR$ (147) CHR$ (144)
50 POKE 53280,1: POKE 53281,1
60 DIM I$(15),A(15)
70 REM ********************
80 REM *** PRINT TITLE ***
90 REM ********************
100 PRINT CHR$ (147) TAB(13)"BUDGET
HELPER"
110 PRINT
120 PRINT "<1> INITIAL AMOUNT:"IA
130 CA = 0: FOR T 2 TO 15
140 CA = CA + A(T): NEXT
150 CA = IA - CA
160 PRINT " CURRENT AMOUNT:"CA
170 PRINT
180 PRINT "EXPENSE ITEMS/AMOUNTS"
190 PRINT
200 REM *************************
210 REM *** PRINT EXPENSES ***
220 REM *************************
230 FOR T = 2 TO 15
240 PRINT T") "I$(T)":"A(T)
250 NEXT
260 REM ******************
270 REM *** GET INPUT***
280 REM ******************
290 PRINT : PRINT "WHICH(1 - 15):";
300 INPUT W$
310 W = VAL (W$)
320 IF W < 1 OR W > 15 THEN 100
330 IF W = 1 THEN 440
340 REM ******************************
350 REM *** ENTER EXPENSE DATA ***
360 REM ******************************
370 PRINT
```

```
380 INPUT "EXPENSE ITEM:";I$(W)
390 INPUT "AMOUNT:";A(W)
400 GOTO 100
410 REM *********************************
420 REM *** ENTER INITIAL AMOUNT ***
430 REM *********************************
440 PRINT
450 INPUT "INITIAL AMOUNT:";IA
460 GOTO 100
```

Section 2

Educational Programs

- Learning the States
- Learning the Capitals
- Math Quizzer
- Trigonometric Functions
- Divisors
- Spelling Practice
- Foreign Language Study
- Graphic Plotter

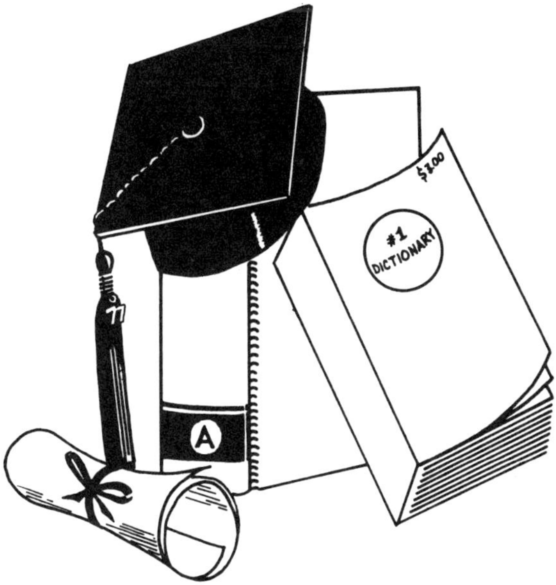

EDUCATIONAL PROGRAMS

Educational software is finally coming into its own. Today, a wider range of software than ever before is available for education. These programs are far more 'learning oriented' than their predecessors. Included in the education section of this book are five extremely useful programs for learning at different levels. The first is Learning the States, a program for memorizing the 50 states of the United States. The second is Learning the Capitals, a program for learning all 50 capitals. Using the Learning the Capitals program I learned the capitals of all 50 states, something I could never seem to do before. Math Quizzer will quiz a student on his addition, subtraction, multiplication and division. For more advanced math, there are programs for finding trigonometric functions and divisors.

Spelling Practice helps students learn to spell lists of words for their spelling quizzes. Any list of words can be entered and they will be flashed back momentarily for a spelling quiz preparation. Finally, for students learning a foreign language, Foreign Language Study will help you remember all those new words. So if you're planning a trip where only Spanish is spoken or if you're trying to pass a vocabulary test, this program will be a patient tutor.

This section is good for learning programs by modification. As you will see, the States and Capitals programs make extensive use of DATA statements. By changing the contents of the DATA statements, students can learn other materials as well. Of course other aspects of the program will have to be changed as well, but only slightly. Use your creativity and see what you can do.

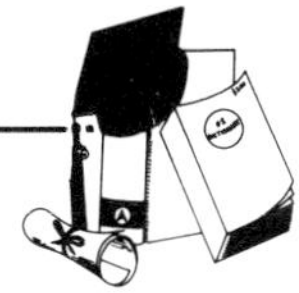

Learning the States

Everyone can recognize the individual states of the United States. But when it comes to reciting all 50 of them from scratch, that's where most people draw the line. Using this program, children can learn to successfully memorize all of the 50 states quickly and have fun doing it. The program is quite simple. Using the menu, for a refresher, you can list all 50 states by typing a 1. Type in a 2 to start the program and a 3 to end it. When putting in the 50 states, you have the option of listing the ones that you have already entered. This is done by entering LIST. You can end the program and get back to the menu by typing END. If you enter all 50 successfully, you win the game!

```
10 REM    **************************
20 REM    ***  SET SCREEN UP ***
30 REM    **************************
40 PRINT CHR$(147)CHR$(144)
50 POKE 53280,1 : POKE 53281,1
60 DIM STATE$(50),ASKED$(50)
70 FOR T=1TO 50 : READ STATE$(T) : NEXT
80 REM    ************************
90 REM    *** PRINT SCREEN ***
100 REM ************************
110 PRINT CHR$(147)TAB(12);
120 PRINT "OUR UNITED STATES"
130 PRINT TAB(12);
140 FOR T=1 TO 17
150 PRINT CHR$(163);
160 NEXT
170 PRINT
180 PRINT
190 PRINT "<1> LIST STATES"
200 PRINT "<2> START"
210 PRINT "<3> QUIT"
220 PRINT : PRINT : PRINT
230 PRINT "END=END"
240 PRINT "LIST=LIST GUESSES"
```

```
250 PRINT CHR$(19) : PRINT : PRINT
260 PRINT : PRINT : PRINT : PRINT
270 INPUT "WHICH :";R$
280 IF VAL (R$)<1 OR VAL(R$)>3 THEN 250
290 IF R$="3"THEN PRINT CHR$(147) : END
300 IF R$<>"1" THEN 460
310 REM **************************************
320 REM *** LOOP & PRINT ALL STATES ***
330 REM **************************************
340 PRINT CHR$(147)
350 FOR T=1 TO 50
360 PRINT STATE$(T)
370 GET R$ : IF R$"" THEN 370
380 NEXT T
390 PRINT: PRINT "THAT'S ALL"
400 GET R$ : IF R$=""THEN 400
410 GOTO 110
420 REM ********************************
430 REM *** ENTER STATE & TELL ***
440 REM *** IF RIGHT OR WRONG  ***
450 REM ********************************
460 PRINT CHR$(147)
470 GUESS=0
480 FOR T=1 TO 50
490 PRINT : PRINT "STATE#";T;
500 GUESS$="" : INPUT ":";GUESS$
510 IF GUESS$="LIST" THEN 820
520 IF GUESS$="END" THEN RUN
530 IF GUESS$="" THEN 490
540 FOR X=1 TO 50
550 IF GUESS$=STATE$(X) THEN 600
560 NEXT
570 PRINT
580 PRINT "THERE'S NO SUCH STATE!"
590 GOTO 490
600 FOR X=1 TO GUESS
610 IF GUESS$=ASKED$(X) THEN 750
620 NEXT
```

```
630 GUESS = GUESS + 1
640 ASKED$(GUESS) = GUESS$
650 NEXT
660 FOR T = 0 TO 255
670 POKE 53280,T : NEXT
680 PRINT : PRINT
690 PRINT "YOU'VE GUESSED THEM ALL!"
700 GET R$ : IF R$ = "" THEN 700
710 RUN
720 REM ****************************************
730 REM ***ALREADY ENTERED BEFORE ***
740 REM ****************************************
750 X = 100
760 PRINT
770 PRINT "ALREADY BEEN USED BEFORE!"
780 GOTO 490
790 REM ******************************
800 REM *** LIST STATES USED ***
810 REM ******************************
820 IF GUESS = 0 THEN 910
830 PRINT
840 FOR X = 1 TO GUESS
850 PRINT "STATE#";X;":";ASKED$(X)
860 GET G$ : IF G$ = "" THEN 860
870 NEXT
880 PRINT : PRINT "THERE'S NO MORE!"
890 GET R$ : IF R$ = "" THEN 890
900 GOTO 490
910 PRINT
920 PRINT "NONE ARE ENTERED YET!"
930 GOTO 490
940 REM ***********************
950 REM *** STATES DATA ***
960 REM ***********************
970 DATA ALABAMA,ALASKA,ARIZONA
980 DATA ARKANSAS,CALIFORNIA,COLORADO
990 DATA CONNECTICUT,DELAWARE
1000 DATA FLORIDA,GEORGIA,HAWAII,IDAHO
```

```
1010 DATA ILLINOIS,INDIANA,IOWA,KANSAS
1020 DATA KENTUCKY
1030 DATA LOUISIANA,MAINE,MARYLAND
1040 DATA MASSACHUSETTS,MICHIGAN
1050 DATA MINNESOTA,MISSISSIPPI
1060 DATA MISSOURI,MONTANA,NEBRASKA
1070 DATA NEVADA,NEW HAMPSHIRE
1080 DATA NEW JERSEY,NEW MEXICO
1090 DATA NEW YORK,NORTH CAROLINA
1100 DATA NORTH DAKOTA,OHIO,OKLAHOMA
1110 DATA OREGON,PENNSYLVANIA
1120 DATA RHODE ISLAND,SOUTH CAROLINA
1130 DATA SOUTH DAKOTA,TENNESSEE,TEXAS
1140 DATA UTAH,VERMONT
1150 DATA VIRGINIA,WASHINGTON
1160 DATA WEST VIRGINIA,WISCONSIN
1170 DATA WYOMING
```

Learning the Capitals

In addition to knowing all 50 states, knowing their respective capitals is equally educational! This program is basically the same as the States program, except that it cannot list the states for which it has already asked you the capitals. You can exit to the menu by typing END in response to a capital entry. It will tell you if your entry is incorrect by printing the state's correct capital when you enter a wrong answer. *Note: Change the dots in line 310 to spaces. They were put there so you don't have to guess as to how many spaces there are.*

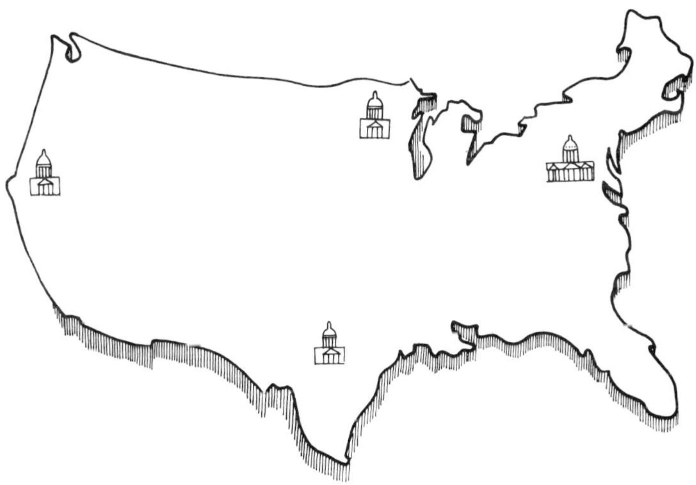

```
10 REM **************************
20 REM *** SET SCREEN UP ***
30 REM **************************
40 PRINT CHR$(147)CHR$(144)
50 POKE 53280,1 : POKE 53281,1
60 DIM ST$(50),CAP$(50),GUESSED(50)
70 FORT=1 TO 50
80 READ ST$(T),CAP$(T)
90 NEXT
100 REM ***********************
110 REM *** PRINT SCREEN***
120 REM ***********************
130 PRINT CHR$(147)TAB(12);
140 PRINT "STATES & CAPITALS"
150 PRINT TAB(12);
151 FOR T=1 TO 17
152 PRINT CHR$(163);
153 NEXT
154 PRINT
160 PRINT : PRINT : PRINT
170 PRINT "<1> LIST STATES & CAPITALS"
180 PRINT "<2> START"
190 PRINT "<3> QUIT"
191 PRINT : PRINT
192 PRINT "END=END"
200 PRINT CHR$(19) : PRINT : PRINT
210 INPUT "WHICH :";R$
220 IF VAL (R$)<1 OR VAL (R$)>3 THEN 200
230 IF R$="3" THEN PRINTCHR$(147) : END
240 IF R$<>"1" THEN 410
250 REM ******************************
260 REM *** LOOP & PRINT ALL    ***
270 REM *** STATES & CAPITALS ***
280 REM ******************************
290 PRINT CHR$(147)
300 FOR T=1 TO 50
310 E$=". . . . . . . . . . ."+ST$(T)
320 PRINT RIGHT$(E$,14);". . .";CAP$(T)
```

```
330 GOSUB 1090
340 NEXT T
350 PRINT : PRINT "THAT'S ALL"
360 GOSUB 1090
370 GOTO 130
380 REM  ************************
390 REM  *** ENTER CAPITAL***
400 REM  ************************
410 PRINT CHR$(147)
420 NUM= INT ( RND (1)*50+1)
430 IF GUESSED(NUM)=1 THEN 420
440 PRINT
450 PRINT "ENTER CAPITAL FOR:";ST$(NUM)
460 GUESS$="" : PRINT"CAPITAL:";
470 INPUT GUESS$
475 IF GUESS$="END" THEN 130
480 IF GUESS$=CAP$(NUM) THEN 520
490 PRINT
500 PRINT "WRONG, IT'S ";CAP$(NUM)
510 GOTO 420
520 PRINT : PRINT "YOU'RE CORRECT!!"
530 GUESSED(NUM)=1
540 FOR T=1 TO 50
550 IF GUESSED(T)=0 THEN T=60
560 NEXT
570 GOTO 420
500 NEXT : PRINT
590 PRINT "YOU'VE DONE THEM ALL!!"
600 GOSUB109 0: RUN
610 REM *******************************
620 REM *** STATE & CAPITAL DATA ***
630 REM *******************************
640 DATA ALABAMA,MONTGOMERY,ALASKA
650 DATA JUNEAU,ARIZONA,PHOENIX
660 DATA ARKANSAS,LITTLE ROCK
670 DATA CALIFORNIA,
SACRAMENTO,COLORADO
680 DATA DENVER,CONNECTICUT,HARTFORD
```

```
690 DATA DELAWARE,DOVER
700 DATA FLORIDA,TALLAHASSEE,GEORGIA
710 DATA ATLANTA,HAWAII,HONOLULU,IDAHO
720 DATA BOISE
730 DATA ILLINOIS,SPRINGFIELD,INDIANA
740 DATA INDIANAPOLIS,IOWA,DES MOINES
750 DATA KANSAS,TOPEKA
760 DATA KENTUCKY,FRANKFORT,LOUISIANA
770 DATA BATON ROUGE,MAINE,AUGUSTA
780 DATA MARYLAND,ANNAPOLIS
790 DATA MASSACHUSETTS,BOSTON,MICHIGAN
800 DATA LANSING
810 DATA MINNESOTA,ST. PAUL,MISSISSIPPI
820 DATA JACKSON,MISSOURI
830 DATA JEFFERSON CITY
840 DATA MONTANA,HELENA,NEBRASKA
850 DATA LINCOLN,NEVADA,CARSON CITY
860 DATA NEW JERSEY,TRENTON
870 DATA NEW HAMPSHIRE,CONCORD
880 DATA NEW MEXICO,SANTA FE,NEW YORK
890 DATA ALBANY
900 DATA NORTH DAKOTA,BISMARCK
910 DATA NORTH CAROLINA,RALIEGH,OHIO
920 DATA COLUMBUS
930 DATA OKLAHOMA,OKLAHOMA
CITY,OREGON
940 DATA SALEM,PENNSYLVANIA,HARRISBURG
950 DATA RHODE ISLAND,PROVIDENCE
960 DATA SOUTH CAROLINA,COLUMBIA
970 DATA SOUTH DAKOTA,PIERRE
980 DATA TEXAS,AUSTIN,TENNESSEE
990 DATA NASHVILLE
1000 DATA UTAH,SALT LAKE CITY,VERMONT
1010 DATA MONTPELIER,VIRGINIA,RICHMOND
1020 DATA WASHINGTON,OLYMPIA
1030 DATA WEST VIRGINIA,CHARLESTON
1040 DATA WISCONSIN,MILWAUKEE
1050 DATA WYOMING,CHEYENNE
```

```
1060 REM *******************
1070 REM *** GET PRESS ***
1080 REM *******************
1090 GET R$ : IFR$ = "" THEN 1090
1100 RETURN
```

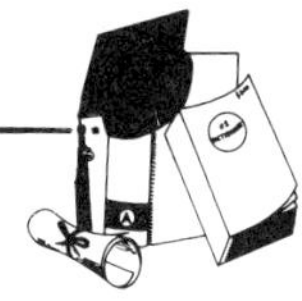

Math Quizzer

The Math Quizzer program was designed to help students who need repetitive review in learning mathematics. With this program, the student can be quizzed in addition, subtraction, multiplication, or division, by entering a number from 1–4. The lower and upper limits from which the computer will pick numbers may also be set. Entering values of 10 and 30 will have the computer pick numbers from 10 to 30 when putting together sample problems. The division option picks out problems with no remainder, as remainders would be quite difficult to do on a computer. If the problem is answered incorrectly, then the correct answer is shown, and a new problem is picked out.

```
10 REM  **********************
20 REM  ***SET SCREEN ***
30 REM  **********************
40 PRINT CHR$(14)CHR$(144)
50 POKE 53280,1 : POKE 53281,1
60 LL=1 : UL=100
70 REM  *************************
80 REM *** PRINT SCREEN   ***
90 REM  *************************
100 PRINT CHR$(147)TAB(15);
110 PRINT "MATH SKILLS"
120 PRINT : PRINT : PRINT "WHICH:"
130 PRINT "<1> ADDITION"
140 PRINT "<2> SUBTRACTION"
150 PRINT "<3> MULTIPLICATION"
160 PRINT "<4> DIVISION"
170 PRINT "<5> SET LIMITS"
180 GET R$ : IF R$="" THEN 180
190 R= VAL (R$)
200 IF R<1 OR R>5 THEN 180
210 IF R=5 THEN 300
220 IF R=2 THEN S$="- "
230 IF R=1 THEN S$="+ "
240 IF R=3 THEN S$="× "
250 IF R=4 THEN S$="/ "
260 GOTO 370
270 REM *********************
280 REM *** SET LIMITS ***
290 REM *********************
300 PRINT : INPUT "LOWER LIMIT:";LL
310 PRINT : INPUT "UPPER LIMIT:";UL
320 NUM=UL-LL+1
330 GOTO 100
340 REM ***************************
350 REM *** TEST ON +,-,/,X ***
360 REM ***************************
370 PRINT CHR$(147)
380 N1 = INT ( RND (1)*NUM+1)+LL-1
```

```
390 IF N1=NM THEN 380
400 N2= INT ( RND (1)*NUM+1)+LL-1
410 IF N2=NN THEN 400
420 IF S$<>"/ " THEN 460
430 IF N2=0 THEN 400
440 FIG=N1/N2
450 IF FIG<> INT (FIG) THEN 380
460 IF S$="- " THEN FIG=N1-N2
470 IF S$="× " THEN FIG=N1*N2
480 IF S$="+ " THEN FIG=N1+N2
490 PRINT : PRINT "WHAT IS "N1;S$;N2"?"
500 ANS$="" : PRINT
510 INPUT "THE ANSWER IS:";ANS$
520 IF ANS$="" THEN 100
530 NM=N1 : NN=N2
540 ANS= VAL (ANS$)
550 PRINT : IF ANS<>FIG THEN 650
560 REM ***********************
570 REM *** YOU'RE RIGHT ***
580 REM ***********************
590 PRINT "RIGHT YOU ARE!"
600 GET R$ : IF R$="" THEN 600
610 GOTO 380
620 REM *************************
630 REM *** YOU'RE WRONG ***
640 REM *************************
650 PRINT "YOU'RE WRONG!. . . .IT'S ";FIG
660 GOTO 600
```

Trigonometric Functions

Having taken quite a few trigonometry courses, I know the importance of having trigonometric functions at your disposal. (Especially since the precision in books usually only goes to about four digits.) With Trigonometric Functions program, you have six basic functions to choose from. Sine, cosine, tangent, cosecant, secant, and cotangent. Simply type the number of the function you want (1-6), and then the computer will prompt you for an angle. Enter the angle (Ø-36Ø), and then the computer will print out the value for whatever function you chose. See, it's easy as 3.14159!

```
1Ø REM *********************
2Ø REM *** SET SCREEN ***
3Ø REM *********************
4Ø PRINT CHR$(147)CHR$(144)
5Ø POKE 5328Ø,1 : POKE 53281,1
6Ø REM *************************
7Ø REM *** PRINT SCREEN ***
8Ø REM *************************
9Ø PRINT CHR$(147)TAB(4)"DERIVING
MATHEMATICAL FUNCTIONS"
1ØØ PRINT TAB(4)"-----------------------------"
11Ø PRINT
12Ø PRINT "<1> SINE"
13Ø PRINT "<2> COSINE"
14Ø PRINT "<3> TANGENT"
15Ø PRINT "<4> COSECANT"
16Ø PRINT "<5> SECANT"
17Ø PRINT "<6> COTANGENT"
18Ø PRINT : PRINT "WHICH:";
19Ø INPUT W$
2ØØ W– VAL (W$)
21Ø IF W<1 OR W>6 THEN 9Ø
22Ø PRINT CHR$(147)"ANGLE(Ø–36Ø):";
23Ø INPUT ANGLE$
24Ø ANGLE= VAL (ANGLE$)
```

```
250 IF ANGLE<0 OR ANGLE>360 THEN 90
260 ANGLE=ANGLE*3.14159/180
270 ON W GOSUB 330,350,370,390,410,430
280 PRINT : PRINT
290 PRINT "THE ANSWER IS "NUM
300 PRINT : PRINT
310 INPUT "PRESS RETURN TO CONTINUE";A$
320 RUN
330 NUM=SIN(ANGLE)
340 RETURN
350 NUM=COS(ANGLE)
360 RETURN
370 NUM=TAN(ANGLE)
380 RETURN
390 NUM=1/SIN(ANGLE)
400 RETURN
410 NUM=1/COS(ANGLE)
420 RETURN
430 NUM=1/TAN(ANGLE)
440 RETURN
```

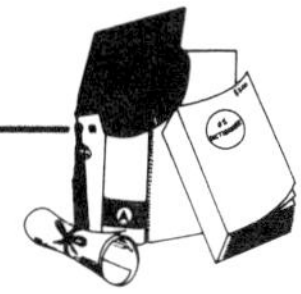

Divisors

Divisors is a program that shows you all of the possible factors of a number. This program is one of the easier ones in this section, so even you beginners should have no problem understanding it. Let's say that you enter the number 8. The computer would print the following:

```
1
2
4
8
```

The program displays the values from one (1) to half of the number you entered. Remember that a divisor of a number cannot be more than half of that number. To be a divisor, the number must divide into your original number without a remainder.

```
10 PRINT CHR$(147)CHR$(144)
20 POKE 53280,1 : POKE 53281,1
30 NUM=0
40 INPUT "ENTER NUMBER";NUM
50 IF NUM=0 THEN PRINT : END
60 FOR T=1 TO NUM/2
70 IF INT(NUM/T)=NUM/T THEN PRINT T
80 NEXT
90 PRINT NUM
100 PRINT
110 GOTO 30
```

Spelling Practice

This is a fun and useful way to prepare for a spelling quiz. When you RUN this program, you will be asked to enter your list of spelling words. After you have entered them all, the words will be given back to you, one at a time, to spell. They are flashed on the screen for just a moment; long enough to recognize the word but not long enough to completely look at it's spelling. You will then be asked to spell the word correctly. If you get the word right, the computer will tell you so. If not, then you will be given more chances until you do get it right.

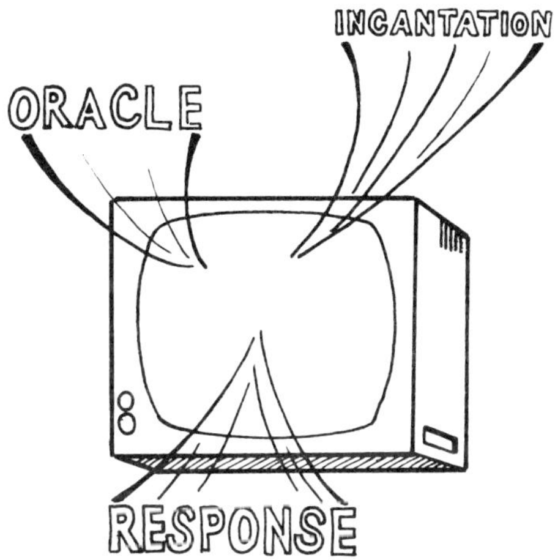

Spelling Practice can be run by the student himself or with his or her parent's help. If parents do help, they should enter the spelling words when the program first asks for the list, and the student can spell them when they flash on the screen. (Also, the words are presented in the reverse order in which they are entered so that they are not memorized in a listed order.) This program has been tested, and students using it improved markedly on their spelling quizzes. See if you can improve your spelling as well!

```
10 REM **********************************
20 REM ** ENTER SPELLING WORDS **
30 REM **********************************
40 PRINT CHR$(147) : CLR: RESTORE : PRINT :
PRINT
50 INPUT "HOW MANY SPELLING WORDS";N
60 PRINT : DIM SP$(N) : PRINT
70 FOR X = 1 TO N
80 PRINT "SPELLING WORD #";X;
90 INPUT SP$(X)
100 NEXT X
200 REM **********************
210 REM ** SPELLING QUIZ **
220 REM **********************
230 FOR X = N TO 1 STEP -1
240 PRINT CHR$ (147)
250 FOR V = 1 TO 10 : PRINT : NEXT V
260 L=LEN(SP$(X)) : PL=20-L/2
270 PRINT CHR$(18); SPC(PL) ;SP$(X)
280 FOR P = 1 TO 200 : NEXT P
290 PRINT CHR$(146); CHR$(147)
300 INPUT "ENTER CORRECT SPELLING ";CS$
310 IF CS$ = SP$(X) THEN 530
320 PRINT : PRINT "+THAT'S NOT QUITE
CORRECT" : PRINT "TRY AGAIN"
330 FOR P = 1 TO 400 : NEXT P
340 PRINT CHR$(147) : GOTO 300
350 NEXT X
360 PRINT : PRINT"ANOTHER SPELLING LIST?(Y/
N)";
370 GET AN$ : IF AN$="" THEN 370
380 IF AN$= "Y" THEN 10
390 PRINT CHR$(147) : FOR V=1 TO
10:PRINT:NEXT V
400 PRINTCHR$(18); SPC(5); "GOOD LUCK ON
YOUR SPELLING TEST!" : END
500 REM *************************
510 REM ** CORRECT ANSWER **
520 REM *************************
```

```
530 PRINTCHR$(147) : FOR I=1 TO 10 : PRINT :
NEXT
540 PRINTCHR$(18); "THAT'S CORRECT!!!"
550 FOR HOLD = 1 TO 500 : NEXT HOLD
560 GOTO 350
```

Foreign Language Study

I remember taking German in high school, with a teacher named Mr. Jose Weill. He was great, but there are some things that a teacher just doesn't have time for. One of these things is repetitive instruction. A computer is perfect for just this sort of thing. German grammar is easy. The difficulty is memorizing the vocabulary. Foreign Language Study eliminates this problem by quizzing you on whatever vocabulary you have entered into a file. It will do this for whatever language you choose. Foreign Language Study is very easy to understand. There are six commands in the main menu:

<1> FILE NAME:XXXXXXX
<2> EDIT VOCABULARY
<3> QUIZ TIME
<4> READ VOCABULARY
<5> WRITE VOCABULARY
<6> QUIT

When the program is first RUN, it will ask you for a file name. Enter something that will remind you of the vocabulary. For instance, say that you are going to enter the vocabulary for the first chapter of your German book. You might wish to call the file: GERMAN–CHAP1. That's just an example though, so do whatever you want. Once that is entered, you can start entering vocabulary. Do this by pressing 2. Now the computer will prompt you with:

```
<1> LIST ENTRIES
<2> ADD TO VOCABULARY
<3> DELETE ENTRIES
<4> RETURN TO MAIN MENU
```

Entering a 4 will return you to the main menu as shown above. To list all of your entries so far, enter a 1. It will ask you if you would like to direct output to the <P>RINTER or to the <S>CREEN. Enter a P or an S. When all of your vocabulary has been listed, the message "THAT'S ALL FOLKS" will be printed, and it will wait for a key to be pressed. Pressing any key will put you into the alternate menu.

Adding entries is easy. Simply enter a 2. Now it will ask you for the English word. Enter, for example, DOG. Next it will ask you for the appropriate foreign word. Enter DER HUND. (That is German for "the dog.") You may have noticed that an X is always printed out. This is done so that if you hit just return, it will put you back into the alternate menu. Feel free to change the string 'foreign' to whatever language you happen to be working with. If you would like to delete an entry, enter a 3, and it will ask you for the entry number to be deleted. Type in the number of the entry you wish to delete, and when you next list the vocabulary, that entry will be gone. Just to be safe, when you are through entering vocabulary for the day enter a 5 at the main menu. This will write all of your entries to disk. Entering a 4 will read those entires into memory. When you are ready to be quizzed on vocabulary, enter a 3 in the main menu. You will now see this menu:

```
<1> ENGLISH TO FOREIGN
<2> FOREIGN TO ENGLISH
<3> RETURN TO MENU
```

If you pick number 1, the computer might say:

```
GIVE ME THE FOREIGN WORD FOR :DOG
```

You would enter DER HUND. The computer will respond with an appropriate answer telling you whether your answer was correct or not. The computer will ask only vocabulary that you have not yet correctly translated. I have found this program to be tremendously helpful as far as memorizing nouns, verbs and such, and I hope you do too.

```
10 REM  *********************
20 REM  *** SET SCREEN ***
30 REM  *********************
40 PRINT CHR$(147)CHR$(144)
50 POKE 53280,1 : POKE 53281,1
60 OPEN 1,0 : C$=CHR$(13)
70 DIM WRD$(1,200),ANS(200)
80 WRDS=0 : BK$=CHR$(157)
90 REM  ************************
100 REM *** PRINT SCREEN ***
110 REM ************************
120 PRINT CHR$(147) TAB(9) "FOREIGN
LANGUAGE STUDY"
130 PRINT : PRINT : PRINT
140 PRINT "MENU:" : PRINT
150 PRINT "<1> FILE NAME:";FILE$
160 PRINT "<2> EDIT VOCABULARY"
170 PRINT "<3> QUIZ TIME"
180 PRINT "<4> READ VOCABULARY"
190 PRINT "<5> WRITE VOCABULARY"
200 PRINT "<6> QUIT"
210 PRINT CHR$(19) : PRINT : PRINT
220 PRINT : PRINT TAB(5);
```

```
230 IF C=0 THEN 340
240 INPUT#1,A$
250 A= VAL (A$)
260 IF A<1 OR A>6 THEN 120
280 ON A GOTO 340,410,1380,1150,1240
290 PRINT CHR$(147)"BYE BYE"
300 END
310 REM ****************************
320 REM *** ENTER FILE NAME ***
330 REM ****************************
340 PRINT CHR$(19) : PRINT : PRINT
350 PRINT : PRINT : PRINT
360 PRINT TAB(14);
370 INPUT#1,FILE$
380 C=1
390 GOTO 120
400 REM **********************
410 REM *** EDIT ENTRIES***
420 REM **********************
430 PRINT CHR$(147)TAB(12)"EDIT
VOCABULARY"
440 PRINT : PRINT
450 PRINT "WHICH:" : PRINT
460 PRINT "<1> LIST VOCABULARY"
470 PRINT "<2> ADD TO VOCABULARY"
480 PRINT "<3> DELETE FROM VOCABULARY"
490 PRINT "<4> RETURN TO MAIN MENU"
500 GET A$ : IF A$="" THEN 500
510 A= VAL (A$)
520 IF A<1 OR A>4 THEN 500
530 ON A GOTO 580,850,1000
540 GOTO 120
550 REM **********************
560 REM *** LIST ENTRIES***
570 REM **********************
580 PRINT CHR$(147)"TO THE <P>RINTER OR
THE <S>CREEN"
590 GET H$ : IF H$="" THEN 590
```

```
600 IF H$<>"P" AND H$<>"S" THEN 430
610 IF H$="S" THEN 650
620 OPEN 2,4
630 PRINT#2,C$C$
640 PRINT#2,TAB(10)"VOCABULARY FOR
"FILE$C$
650 IF WRDS=0 THEN 800
660 PRINT
670 FOR T=0 TO WRDS-1
680 T$=RIGHT$("  "+STR$(T+1),3)
690 IF H$="S" THEN 710
700 PRINT#2,T$":"WRD$(0,T),,WRD$(1,T)
710 PRINT T$":"WRD$(0,T) TAB(20) WRD$(1,T)
720 IF PEEK(197)<>60 THEN 760
730 X=PEEK(197)
740 IF X=64 THEN 730
750 IF X<>60 THEN T=500
760 NEXT
770 PRINT : PRINT "THAT'S ALL FOLKS!"
780 GET R$ : IF R$="" THEN 780
790 CLOSE 2 : GOTO 430
800 PRINT : PRINT "THERE'S NONE ENTERED!"
810 GOTO 780
820 REM  ********************
830 REM  *** ADD WORDS ***
840 REM  ********************
850 PRINT CHR$(147)TAB(13)"ADD
VOCABULARY"
860 PRINT : PRINT
870 PRINT : PRINT
880 W$=RIGHT$("  "+STR$(WRDS+1),3)
890 PRINT "ENGLISH WORD#"W$":X"BK$;
900 INPUT#1,EW$
910 IF EW$="X" THEN 430
920 PRINT : PRINT "FOREIGN WORD#"W":X"BK$;
930 INPUT#1,FW$
940 IF FW$="X" THEN 430
950 WRD$(0,WRDS)=EW$ :
```

```
WRD$(1,WRDS)=FW$
960 WRDS=WRDS+1 : GOTO 870
970 REM ************************
980 REM *** DELETE ENTRY ***
990 REM ************************
1000 PRINT CHR$(147)TAB(11)"DELETE
VOCABULARY"
1010 PRINT : PRINT
1020 PRINT
1030 PRINT "ENTRY TO DELETE:";
1040 INPUT#1,D1
1050 IF D1>WRDS+1 THEN 430
1060 FOR T=D1 TO WRDS-1
1070 WRD$(0,T-1)=WRD$(0,T)
1080 WRD$(1,T-1)=WRD$(1,T)
1090 NEXT
1100 WRDS=WRDS-1
1110 GOTO 430
1120 REM ****************************
1130 REM *** READ VOCABULARY ***
1140 REM ****************************
1150 OPEN 5,8,5,"0:"+FILE$+",S,R"
1160 WRDS=0
1170 INPUT#5,WRD$(0,WRDS),WRD$(1,WRDS)
1180 IF WRD$(0,WRDS)="EOF" THEN 1200
1190 WRDS=WRDS+1 : GOTO 1170
1200 CLOSE 5 : GOTO 120
1210 REM *****************************
1220 REM *** WRITE VOCABULARY ***
1230 REM *****************************
1240 OPEN 15,8,15
1250 PRINT#15,"S0:"+FILE$
1260 CLOSE 15
1270 OPEN 5,8,5,"0:"+FILE$+",S,W"
1280 IF WRDS=0 THEN 1320
1290 FOR T=0 TO WRDS-1
1300 PRINT#5,WRD$(0,T)C$WRD$(1,T)
1310 NEXT
```

```
1320 PRINT#5,"EOF"C$"EOF"
1330 CLOSE 5
1340 GOTO 120
1350 REM *******************
1360 REM *** QUIZ TIME ***
1370 REM *******************
1380 PRINT CHR$(147)TAB(15)"QUIZ TIME"
1390 PRINT : PRINT : PRINT
1400 PRINT "<1> ENGLISH TO FOREIGN"
1410 PRINT "<2> FOREIGN TO ENGLISH"
1420 PRINT "<3> RETURN TO MENU"
1430 PRINT
1440 PRINT "WHICH:";
1450 INPUT#1,A$
1460 A= VAL (A$)
1470 IF A<1 OR A>3 THEN 1380
1480 IF A=3 THEN 430
1490 PRINT CHR$(147)
1500 FOR T=0 TO WRDS-1
1510 ANS(T)=0 : NEXT
1520 A$="ENGLISH" : ANS=0 : WO=1
1530 IF A=1 THEN A$"FOREIGN" : ANS=1 :
WO=0
1540 NUM=INT(RND(1)*WRDS)
1550 IF ANS(NUM)=1 THEN 1540
1560 PRINT "GIVE ME THE "A$" WORD FOR
"WRD$(WO,NUM)
1570 PRINT "ANSWER:";
1580 INPUT#1,ANS$
1590 IF ANS$="X" THEN 120
1600 PRINT
1610 IF ANS$<>WRD$(ANS,NUM) THEN 1710
1620 PRINT "CORRECT!" : PRINT
1630 ANS(NUM)=1
1640 FOR S=0 TO WRDS-1
1650 IF ANS(S)=1 THEN NEXT : GOTO 1760
1660 S=500 : NEXT
1670 GOTO 1540
```

```
1680 REM *************************
1690 REM *** WRONG ANSWER ***
1700 REM *************************
1710 PRINT "WRONG, IT'S "WRD$(ANS,NUM)
1720 PRINT : GOTO 1540
1730 REM **********************************
1740 REM *** ANSWERED ALL OF THEM ***
1750 REM **********************************
1760 PRINT : PRINT
1770 PRINT "YOU'VE ANSWERED ALL OF THEM
CORRECTLY!"
1780 GET R$ : IF R$="" THEN 1780
1790 GOTO 120
```

Graphic Plotter

In order to use the fabulous graphics that the COMMODORE 64 is capable of producing, it is necessary to use POKEs (in BASIC), machine language programs, or assemblers. Graphics are great for machine language, but not so great if you're working in BASIC.

To me, one of the most exciting things a computer can do is produce graphs. Bar graphs can be done with graphic characters, but for the precision needed with mathematical functions, hi-res graphics is the only solution.

Here's how to work the program. The first question that the computer asks you is whether or not you would like to clear the hi-res screen. This is available in case you would like to plot your function over a picture already in memory. Next it asks you if you would like a set of axes drawn on the screen which is sometimes useful in plotting lots of numbers. When the plot is over, it waits for you to press a key. The program will then put you back into text mode. From this point, you can RUN the hi-res program, and SAVE your function disk. The clear routine is the same one as used in the hi-res drawing program. To change the height of the graph, you must change the amplitude. The variable amplitude is located in line 30. Changing it changes the height of the graph. You can use negative numbers if you wish. An effect that really looks nice is to put in a FOR-NEXT loop in line 240 that varies the amplitude from −1 to 1, by STEP .1. It gives a very good 3-D effect. To change the period of the graph, divide the variable domain in line 250, by some number. My graphing program will use a domain from −2 Pi to 2 Pi. If you would like a COS plot, then merely change the SIN in line 250 to COS. It's as easy as that! For other ideas for equations, consult page 394 in the *Commodore 64 Programmer's Reference Guide.*

```
10 PRINT CHR$(147)CHR$(144)
20 POKE 53280,0 : POKE 53281,1
25 PI=3.14
30 CLEAR=51712 : AMPLITUDE=1
40 FOR T=51712 TO 51738
50 READ P : POKE T,P : NEXT
60 PRINT CHR$(147)TAB(13)"FUNCTION PLOT"
70 PRINT : PRINT : PRINT
80 INPUT "CLEAR THE HI-RES SCREEN(Y/N):";C$
90 IF C$<>"Y" AND C$<>"N" THEN 80
100 INPUT "DRAW A SET OF AXES(Y/N):";D$
110 IF D$<>"Y" AND D$<>"N" THEN 100
120 GOSUB 390
130 IF C$ = "N" THEN 180
140 POKE 251,0 : POKE 252,32
150 POKE 253,63 : POKE 254,63
160 POKE 51715,0
170 SYS CLEAR
180 IF D$="N" THEN 240
190 FOR T=12036 TO 12348 STEP 8
200 POKE T,255 : NEXT
210 FOR T=8352 TO 16032 STEP 320
220 FOR S=0 TO 7
230 POKE T+S,PEEK(T+S)OR128 : NEXT : NEXT
240 FOR DOMAIN=-2*PI TO 2*PI
250 Y=AMPLITUDE*SIN(DOMAIN)*60+100
260 X=DOMAIN*25+160
270 Y=200-Y
280 BY=8192+INT(Y/8)*320+8*INT(X/
8)+(YAND7)
290 BI=7-(XAND7)
300 POKE BY,PEEK(BY)OR(2^BI)
310 NEXT
320 GET R$ : IF R$="" THEN 320
330 GOSUB 500
340 PRINT "THE PLOT IS DONE"
350 END
```

```
360 REM  **************
370 REM *** HI-RES ***
380 REM  **************
390 PRINT CHR$(147)
400 POKE 53272,PEEK(53272)OR 8
410 POKE 53265,PEEK(53265)OR 32
420 POKE 251,0 : POKE 252,4
430 POKE 253,231 : POKE 254,7
440 POKE 51715,1
450 SYS CLEAR
460 RETURN
470 REM  ************
480 REM  *** TEXT ***
490 REM  ************
500 PRINT CHR$(147)
510 POKE 53272,21
520 POKE 53265,27
530 POKE 198,0
540 RETURN
550 REM  ************************
560 REM *** MEMORY CLEAR ***
570 REM  ************************
580 DATA 160,0,169,0,145,251,166,252
590 DATA 228,254,144,7,166,251,228
600 DATA 253,144,1,96,230,251,208,237
610 DATA 230,252,208,233
```

Section 3

Entertainment Programs

- Pick A Number
- Planet Lander
- Death Hunt
- Guided Missile Commander
- Drawing Machine
- Adventure Character Creator
- Unknown Crypt
- Stereo Graphic

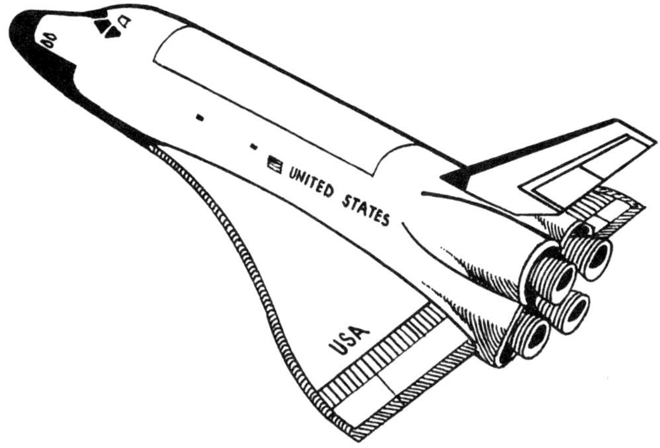

ENTERTAINMENT PROGRAMS

For the entertainment section of this book, I wanted to give an example of the three ways of programming games on the COMMODORE 64. Included are one game using text characters, one using programmable characters, and one using the COMMODORE 64's sprites. The game Death Hunt uses only text and graphics characters. Guided Missile Commander uses programmable characters, characters which are redefined from the COMMODORE character set. Planet Lander uses sprites. Sprites are an extremely quick way of putting block graphics on the screen.

Two other programs in this section are Pick A Number, where the computer generates a random number that the user has to guess, and Drawing Machine, a program that allows the user to create and edit a high-resolution picture. The picture can be SAVEd to disk, and then later recalled. The next two programs, Adventure Character Creator and Unknown Crypt, provide a computerized means of creating adventure characters and mazes for role-playing games. It takes the tedious work out of such games, leaving more time to enjoy the game and less time to deal with the paper work. Finally, a little program, Stereo Graphic, shows the combination of graphics and the internal clock in the COMMODORE 64. It is a nifty little surprise.

Look to see how the programs produce animation and how graphic characters are generated. There are hints in all of these programs on how arcade games are created. Who knows? Someday you may make your own!

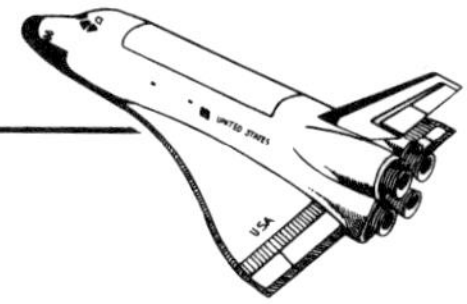

Pick A Number

Just about every child enjoys playing guessing games. For those of you new to programming, it is a good place to start understanding how games are made using random numbers. You may want to enhance it, but in the meantime, young children will enjoy it immensely as it is.

Pick A Number randomly selects a number from 1–100, and asks you to choose the number it has picked. The computer tells you if your guess is too low or too high. Should you win, the computer screen flashes in a variety of colors. After each wrong guess, you must press a key to guess again. The number of guesses is posted at the end of the game. See if you can determine the maximum strategy for deducing the computer's number. (If you play the Numbers, do not use this program!)

```
10 REM  **********************
20 REM  *** SET SCREEN***
30 REM  **********************
40 PRINT CHR$(147)CHR$(144)
50 POKE 53280,1
60 POKE 53281,1
70 REM **************************
80 REM *** PRINT SCREEN ***
90 REM **************************
100 ANS= INT ( RND (1)*100+1) : G=0
110 GOSUB 390
120 PRINT CHR$(19) : PRINT
130 PRINT "GUESS IT:";
140 GUESS$=""
150 INPUT GUESS$
160 IF GUESS$="" THEN 110
170 G=G+1
180 GUESS= VAL (GUESS$)
190 IF GUESS<1 OR GUESS>100 THEN 570
200 IF GUESS<ANS THEN 320
210 IF GUESS=ANS THEN 650
220 REM  *******************************
230 REM  *** GUESS IS > ANSWER ***
240 REM  *******************************
250 PRINT : PRINT "TOO HIGH!"
260 GOSUB 460
270 GOSUB 510
280 GOTO 110
290 REM  *******************************
300 REM  *** GUESS IS< ANSWER **
310 REM  *******************************
320 PRINT : PRINT "TOO LOW!"
330 GOSUB 460
340 GOSUB 510
350 GOTO 110
360 REM ******************************
370 REM *** PRINT TOP BORDER ***
380 REM ******************************
```

```
390 PRINT CHR$(147)TAB(14);
400 PRINT "NUMBER GUESS"
410 PRINT TAB(14)"----------------- "
420 RETURN
430 REM *******************
440 REM *** GET PRESS ***
450 REM *******************
460 GET R$ : IF R$="" THEN 460
470 RETURN
480 REM ***************************
490 REM *** POSITION CURSOR ***
500 REM ***************************
510 PRINT CHR$(19) : PRINT : PRINT
520 PRINT : PRINT
530 RETURN
540 REM *************************
550 REM *** OUT OF BOUNDS ***
560 REM *************************
570 PRINT
580 PRINT "OUT OF BOUNDS. . . . 1-100!"
590 GOSUB 460
600 GOSUB 510
610 GOTO 110
620 REM ********************
630 REM *** GUESSED IT ***
640 REM ********************
650 PRINT
660 PRINT "YOU GOT IT IN"G" GUESSES!"
670 FOR T=0 TO 255
680 POKE 53281,T : NEXT
690 POKE 53281,1
700 GOSUB 460
710 RUN
```

Planet Lander

Sprites are an extremely powerful enhancement to the COMMODORE 64. They can be used for animation in games, or be put to use for a variety of other purposes. Planet Lander uses a sprite to depict a rocket making a landing on an alien planet. The action is extremely smooth and fast, something that few other computers can boast. Your mission, should you decide to accept it, is to navigate your rocket around the many asteroids (%$#&!) on the planet and land safely on the surface. To make a successful landing, you must have a horizontal acceleration of zero, and a vertical acceleration of less than seven tenths (.7). Both of these movement speeds are constantly shown on the upper portion of the screen. To control your thrust, hit the space bar. To activate your retro–rockets, to negate that thrust, press the R key. The keys J and L activate the left and right components of your horizontal acceleration, and the K key has a neutralizing affect. If you either crash or land, the appropriate message will be printed on the screen. When you press the RETURN key, you will be asked if you wish to play again.

```
10 REM **************************
20 REM *** PLANET LANDER ***
30 REM **************************
40 PRINT CHR$(147)CHR$(144)
50 POKE 53280,1 : POKE 53281,1
60 BA=1024 : CA=55296 : S=42 : E=53269
70 POKE E,0 : C0=53279 : POKE C0,0
80 FOR T=1 TO 22 : PRINT : NEXT
90 FOR T=1 TO 40
100 PRINT "8"; : NEXT
110 PRINT CHR$(19)
120 FOR M=1 TO 20
130 MX= INT ( RND (1)*38)
140 MY= INT ( RND (1)*12+5)
150 POKE BA+40*MY+MX,S
160 POKE CA+40*MY+MX,0
170 NEXT
```

```
180 PRINT CHR$(19)
190 FOR J=0 TO 62
200 READ X : POKE 832+J,X
210 NEXT : POKE 832+J,0
220 FOR J=0 TO 62
230 READ X : POKE 896+J,X
240 NEXT : POKE 896+J,0
250 X0=53248 : Y0=53249
260 X1=53250 : Y1=53251
270 POKE 2040,13 : POKE 2041,14
280 POKE 53287,0 : POKE 53288,2
290 POKE 53271,0 : POKE 53277,0
300 POKE C0,0
310 V=70 : H=24 : V0=0 : H0=0
320 POKE X0,H : POKE Y0,V
330 POKE X1,H : POKE Y1,V+4
340 POKE 53269,1
350 K=PEEK(203) : GET K$
360 IF K$="" THEN 460
370 K0=ASC(K$) : V1=.1 : H1=0
380 E0=1 : IF K0=32 THEN V1=-.5 : E0=3
390 IF K0=74 THEN H1=-.2
400 IF K0=76 THEN H1=.2
410 IF K0=75 AND H0>0 THEN H0=H0-.2
420 IF K0=75 AND H0<0 THEN H0=H0+.2
430 IF K0=75 THEN H1=0
440 IF K0=82 THEN V1=.2
450 GOTO 470
460 IF K=64 THEN V1=.1 : H1=0 : E0=1
470 V0=V0+V1 : H0=H0+H1
480 IF V<65 THEN V0=ABS(V0)
490 IF H<23 THEN H0=ABS(H0)
500 IF H>320 THEN H0=-ABS(H0)
530 V=V+V0 : H=H+H0
540 IF V<V0 THEN POKE E,3 : GOTO 560
550 POKE E,E0
560 VO=V
570 HI=INT(H/256):LO=H-256*HI
```

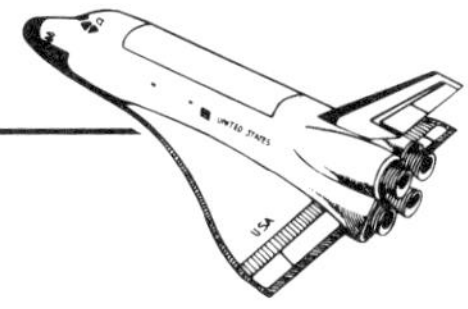

```
580 POKE 53264,HI*3#
590 POKE X0, LO : POKE Y0,V
600 POKE X1, LO: POKE Y1, V+4
610 V0= VAL ( LEFT$ ( STR$ (V0),4))
620 H0= VAL ( LEFT$ ( STR$ (H0),4))
630 PRINT CHR$(19)TAB(12)"                    ";
640 PRINT TAB(31)"                    "
650 PRINTCHR$(19)"VERT. ACC.:"V0;
660 PRINT TAB(20)"HOR. ACC.:"H0
670 C=PEEK(C0)
680 IF (C AND 1)=0 THEN 350
690 IF V<75 THEN 350
700 IF V>185 THEN 760
710 S$="YOU'VE CRASHED INTO A METEOR!"
720 GOTO 1140
730 REM ****************************
740 REM *** CHECK LANDING ***
750 REM ****************************
760 S$="YOU'VE CRASHED ON THE MOON!"
770 IF V0>.6 OR H0<>0 THEN 1140
780 S$="SUCCESSFUL LANDING!"
790 GOTO 1040
800 REM ************************
810 REM ***PLANET DATA ***
820 REM ************************
830 DATA 159,255,249,90,0,6,72,190,250
840 DATA 136,160,137,136,160,137,136
850 DATA 190,249,136
860 DATA 130,137,136,130,137,136,130
870 DATA 137,79,190,138,32,0,4,25,255
880 DATA 152,9,85,144
890 DATA 9,170,144,17,255,136,32,0,4,32
900 DATA 126,4,32,129,4,129,252,127
910 DATA 195,254,255,231,255
920 REM ***********************
930 REM *** FLAME DATA ***
940 REM ***********************
950 DATA 0,0,0,0,0,0,0,0,0,0,0,0,0,0,0
```

```
960 DATA 0,0,0,0,0,0,0,0,0,0,0,0,0,0,0
970 DATA 0,0,0
980 DATA 0,0,0,0,0,0,0,0,0,0,0,0,0,0,0
990 DATA 0,0,0,63,129,252,31,0,248,14,0
1000 DATA 112,4,0,32
1010 REM *************************
1020 REM *** GOOD LANDING ***
1030 REM *************************
1040 PRINT CHR$(19) : PRINT S$
1050 GET R$ : IF R$<>CHR$(13) THEN 1050
1060 POKE E,0 : PRINT CHR$(147)
1070 PRINT "ANOTHER GAME (Y/N)"
1080 GET R$ : IF R$="" THEN 1080
1090 IF R$="Y " THEN RUN
1100 END
1110 REM ***********************
1120 REM *** BAD LANDING ***
1130 REM ***********************
1140 B=832
1150 FOR T=1 TO 50
1160 AM= INT ( RND (1)*6)
1170 V=V+AM
1180 POKE Y0,V
1190 POKE Y1,V
1200 IF V>210 THEN V=210
1210 POKE Y0,V : POKE Y1,V
1220 NEXT
1230 GOTO 1040
```

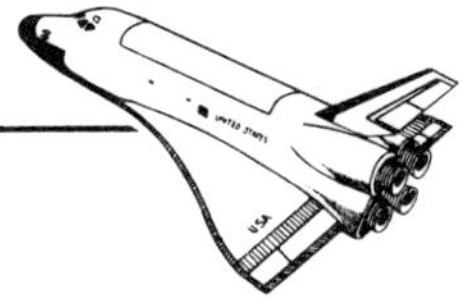

Death Hunt!

The COMMODORE 64 supports quite a nice character set, including upper case, lower case, and even graphic characters. These graphic symbols are nice because they add flair to any program, whether they're used for a border or for a game charcter. Death Hunt! is an example of a text-character game. In it, I used graphic characters instead of sprites or programmable characters to represent the game pieces. The object of the game is to manuever your circle around the screen, bumping into the black dot, (the enemy) being careful not to hit the mines (represented by X's) or the tombstones left behind by the deaths of your enemies. Try to collect as many points as you can before you get zapped.

```
10 REM **********************************
20 REM *** SET SCREEN & VARIABLES ***
30 REM **********************************
40 PRINT CHR$(147)CHR$(144)
50 PRINT CHR$(142)CHR$(8)
60 P1=53280 : P2=53281
70 B3=2023 : SP=32 : B1=1064 : B2=55336
80 CH=87 : EN=81 : CR=88 : MI=86
90 POKE 649,1 : AM=54272
100 PRINTCHR$(147)"SCORE:"SC
110 POKE P1,1 : POKE P2,1 : O=1 : F=40
120 FOR T=1 TO 100
130 PL= INT ( RND (1)*960)
140 POKE B1+PL,MI : POKE B2+PL,0
150 NEXT
160 PP=B1 : P$=""
170 EP=1264+ INT ( RND (1)*760) : P$=""
180 REM *********************
190 REM ** START GAME ***
200 REM *********************
210 POKE PP,CH : POKE PP+AM,0
220 POKE EP,EN : POKE EP+AM,0
230 GET R$
```

```
240 IF R$="" AND P$="" THEN 370
250 IF R$="" THEN R$=P$
260 P$=R$
270 M=0
280 IF R$="J" THEN M=-O
290 IF R$="L" THEN M=O
300 IF R$="K" THEN M=F
310 IF R$="I" THEN M=-F
320 IF M=0 THEN P$="" : GOTO 370
330 IF PP+M<B1 OR PP+M>B3 THEN 370
340 L= PEEK (PP+M)
350 IF L<>32 AND L<>0 THEN 530
360 POKE PP,SP : PP=PP+M
370 X= INT ( RND (1)*4)
380 IF X=0 THEN M=O
390 IF X=1 THEN M=-O
400 IF X=2 THEN M=F
410 IF X=3 THEN M=-F
420 E = PEEK (EP+M)
430 IF E<>SP AND E<>CH THEN 370
440 POKE EP,SP : EP=EP+M
450 IF EP>B3 THEN EP=B3
460 IF EP<B1 THEN EP=B1
470 POKE EP,EN : POKE EP+AM,0
480 IF PP=EP THEN 540
490 GOTO 210
500 REM ******************
510 REM *** COLLISION ***
520 REM ******************
530 IF L<>EN THEN 710
540 FOR T=1 TO 3
550 POKE PP+M,CR+128
560 FOR S=1 TO 100
570 NEXT
580 POKE PP+M,CR
590 FOR S=1 TO 100
600 NEXT
610 NEXT
```

```
620 SC = SC + 1
630 PRINT CHR$(19)TAB(7)SC
640 P$ = ""
650 EP = 1264 + INT ( RND (1)*760)
660 IF PEEK (EP)<>32 THEN 650
670 GOTO 210
680 REM *******************
690 REM *** MUNCH IT ***
700 REM *******************
710 FOR T = 0 TO 255
720 POKE P1,T : POKE P2,T
730 NEXT
740 POKE P1,1 : POKE P2,1
750 PRINT CHR$(147)"YOU MUNCHED IT!!"
760 PRINT : PRINT : PRINT
770 PRINT "PLAY AGAIN (Y/N)"
780 GET R$ : IF R$ = "" THEN 780
790 IF R$ = "Y" THEN RUN
800 PRINT : PRINT : PRINT "SO LONG. . . ."
```

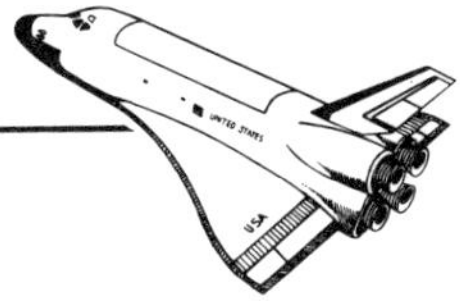

Guided Missile Commander

Programmable characters are an extremely powerful feature of the VIC-20 and COMMODORE 64 computers. They can be used for designing foreign character sets, or simply for making odd shapes to use in games. Character Create, a program included in this book, was employed for making programmable characters as well as saving a good deal of programming time.

The main thrust behind Guided Missile Commander is to kill as many invading alien pods as possible in under thirty seconds. A timer in the upper right portion of the screen constantly reminds you of the time remaining. In the upper left hand of the screen is your current score. Aliens will come shooting across the screen in a horizontal motion, at random levels, subject to your missile fire. The two arrow keys control your gun's horizontal movement, and the space bar fires your heat-seeking missile. Once a missile is fired, the cursor keys control the horizontal position of that missile, not of your gun turret.

To end a missile's flight before it goes off the screen, simply press the space bar, and a new missile will take place of the old one at the bottom of the screen. If you wish to end a missile's flight without launching another missile, simply press Q. At the end of the game, the computer will tell you your score. Good luck in shooting the invaders from outer space!

```
10 REM  *********************
20 REM  *** SET SCREEN ***
30 REM  *********************
40 PRINT CHR$(147)CHR$(144)CHR$(142)
60 POKE 53280,1 : POKE 53281,1
70 POKE 52,48 : POKE 56,48 : CLR
80 POKE 56334, PEEK (56334) AND 254
90 POKE 1, PEEK (1) AND 251
100 FOR I=0 TO 535
110 POKE I+12288, PEEK (I+53248)
120 NEXT
130 POKE 1, PEEK (1) OR 4
140 POKE 56334, PEEK (56334) OR 1
150 T=( PEEK (53272) AND 240)+12
160 POKE 53272,T
170 BA=1064 : AM=54272
180 PB=1984 : PC=2023
190 REM ************************
200 REM *** GET SHIP DATA ***
210 REM ************************
220 FOR T=0 TO 7
230 READ C
240 POKE 12288+T,C
250 NEXT
260 DATA 195,60,24,24,24,24,255,255
270 REM ***************************
280 REM *** GET BULLET DATA ***
290 REM ***************************
300 FOR T=0 TO 7
310 READ C
```

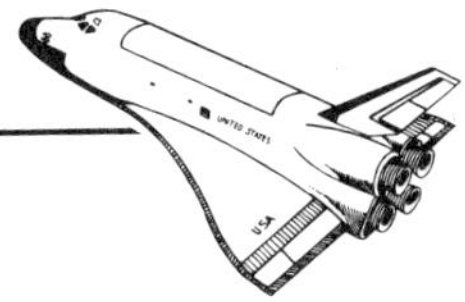

```
320 POKE 12296+T,C
330 NEXT
340 DATA 16,16,16,40,40,40,108,130
350 REM ****************************
360 REM *** GET ENEMY DATA ***
370 REM ****************************
380 FOR T=0 TO 7
390 READ C
400 POKE 12304+T,C
410 NEXT
420 DATA 0,0,0,60,66,255,66,60
430 REM **************************
440 REM *** GET SPACE DATA ***
450 REM **************************
460 FOR T=0 TO 7
470 POKE 12320+T,0
480 NEXT
490 REM **********************
500 REM *** START GAME ***
510 REM **********************
520 PRINT CHR$(147)"SCORE:";
530 PRINT TAB(30)"TIME:"
540 PP= 2003: TI$="000000" : AN=0
550 SC=0
560 MP=PP : MS=0
570 Y= INT ( RND (1)*12+ 1) : AN=AN+1
580 EP=BA+40*Y : ES=EP
590 POKE EP,2 : POKE EP+AM,0
600 POKE PP,0 : POKE PP+AM,0
610 K= PEEK (197)
620 T$=RIGHT$(TI$,2)
630 T$=RIGHT$("0"+STR$(30-VAL(T$)),2)
640 IF VAL(T$)<0 THEN 1100
650 PRINT CHR$(19)TAB(35)T$
660 IF K<>7 AND K<>2 THEN 690
670 IF MS=1 THEN 690
680 POKE PP,4
690 IF MS=1 THEN POKE MP,4 : GOTO 720
```

```
700 IF K=7 AND PP>PB THEN PP=PP-1
710 IF K=2 AND PP<PC THEN PP=PP+1
720 IF K=7 AND PP>PB THEN MP=MP-1
730 IF K=2 AND PP<PC THEN MP=MP+1
740 IF K=60 THEN MS=1
750 IF K=60 OR K=62 THEN MP=PP
760 IF K=62 THEN MS=0 : GOTO 860
770 IF K<>7 AND K<>2 THEN 800
780 POKE PP-1,4
790 POKE PP,0 : POKE PP+AM,0
800 IF MS=0 THEN 860
810 MP=MP-40
820 IF MP<BA THEN MP=PP : MS=0
830 IF MP<BA THEN 860
840 IF PEEK (MP)=2 THEN 930
850 POKE MP,1 : POKE MP+AM,0
860 POKE EP,4 : EP=EP+1
870 IF EP>ES+39 THEN 570
880 POKE EP,2: POKE EP+AM,0
890 GOTO 610
900 REM *******************
910 REM *** ENEMY HIT ***
920 REM *******************
930 FOR T=1 TO 10
940 POKE MP,1
950 FOR S=1 TO 30
960 NEXT
970 POKE MP,2
980 FOR S=1 TO 30
990 NEXT
1000 NEXT
1010 POKE MP,4
1020 POKE 197,64
1030 POKE PP,4
1040 SC=SC+1
1050 PRINT CHR$(19)TAB(6)SC
1060 GOTO 560
```

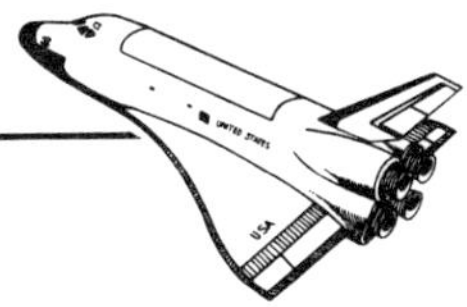

```
1070 REM **********************
1080 REM *** OUT OF TIME ***
1090 REM **********************
1100 FOR T=1 TO 20
1110 POKE PP,4
1120 FOR S=1 TO 50
1130 NEXT
1140 POKE PP,0
1150 FOR S=1 TO 50
1160 NEXT
1170 NEXT
1180 PRINT CHR$(147); : POKE 53272,21
1190 PRINT "YOU'RE OUT OF TIME!"
1200 PRINT
1210 PRINT"YOU KILLED"SC"OUT OF"AN;
1220 PRINT "POSSIBLE!"
1230 PRINT
1240 PRINT "PLAY AGAIN (Y/N)"
1250 POKE 198,0 : POKE 197,64
1260 GET R$ : IF R$="" THEN 1260
1270 IF R$="N" THEN END
1280 IF R$<>"Y" THEN 1260
1290 PRINT CHR$(147)
1300 T=( PEEK (53272) AND 240)+12
1310 POKE 53272,T
1320 GOTO 520
```

Drawing Machine

Of all the programs in the book, my personal favorite is the Drawing Machine. It took a lot of programming time to create, but it was worth the effort. Using this program, you can draw, erase, save and recall hi-resolution pictures. Each picture takes up 32 blocks on disk. Another powerful feature is the ability to lay one picture on top of another. You can draw a picture, save it to disk, then draw another picture, and by specifying a file name, have that file laid right on top of the one you're currently editing. It meshes them right together! Using the joystick in port 2, you can draw in just about every direction. The program even has a sprite in the shape of a pencil to show you where you are currently drawing. Many of these routines are put in machine language for speed. They are integrated into the BASIC program, so you don't need an assembler or monitor to include them.

You can choose from two colors, white and black (real exciting, huh!). White is selected by typing 2, and black by a 1. Drawing is achieved by holding down the joystick button and moving it at the same time. Just moving the joystick will move the pencil without plotting. To recall a drawing, type F 1. Your drawings must be from 1–12 characters in length, because a suffix of .PIC is added to all file names to distinguish them from other files. Hit RETURN if you do not wish to recall a file, and it will place you back in the draw mode. To SAVE a picture, type F3. It too, will prompt you for a file name of the same length. Hit RETURN if you do not wish to SAVE your picture. To clear the screen, and start off fresh, press SHIFT CLR/HOME. (Be careful with this one.) You may also MERGE a picture on disk with whatever you have in memory. Simply type M, and you will be prompted with a file name. Type it in and wait for it to load. Once it is in a different section of memory, the MERGE process takes place. In a matter of less than a second, the two pictures are MERGEd together as one. Due to the plotting portion of the program being in BASIC, the drawing can be quite slow sometimes, but hang in there!

```
10 PRINT CHR$ (147) CHR$ (144)
20 V = 53248: POKE 2040,13
30 POKE V + 29,0: POKE V + 23,0
40 POKE 53280,0: POKE 53281,1
50 CLEAR = 51829
60 SL – 51712:MERG = 51780
70 FOR T = 51712 TO 51855
80 READ P: POKE T,P: NEXT
90 FOR N = 0 TO 62: READ Q
100 POKE 832 + N,Q: NEXT
110 M = 0:JOY = 56320
120 GOSUB 670
130 POKE 251,0: POKE 252,32
140 POKE 253,63: POKE 254,63
150 POKE 51832,0
160 SYS CLEAR
170 X = 160:Y = 100
```

```
180 POKE V,X + 21: POKE V + 1,Y + 30
190 POKE V + 39,11: POKE V + 21,1
200 POKE 650,128
210 REM *******************
220 REM *** GET INPUT ***
230 REM *******************
240 J = NOT PEEK (JOY) AND 15
250 B = - (( PEEK (JOY) AND 16) = 0)
260 R = PEEK (197)
270 IF B THEN 370
280 IF B OR J THEN 520
290 IF R = 64 THEN 240
300 IF R = 4 THEN 860
310 IF R = 5 THEN 950
320 IF R = 36 THEN 1080
330 IF R = 51 THEN 130
340 IF R = 56 THEN M = 0: POKE 53280,M
350 IF R = 59 THEN M = 1: POKE 53280,M
360 IF R = 56 OR R = 59 THEN 240
370 IF J AND 1 AND Y > 0 THEN Y = Y - 1
380 IF J AND 2 AND Y < 199 THEN Y = Y + 1
390 IF J AND 4 AND X > 0 THEN X = X - 1
400 IF J AND 8 AND X < 319 THEN X = X + 1
410 HI = INT ((X + 21) / 256)
420 POKE V + 16,HI
430 POKE V,X + 21 - 256 * HI
440 POKE V + 1,Y + 30
450 BY = 8192 + INT (Y / 8) * 320 + 8 * INT (X /
8) + (Y AND 7)
460 BI = 7 - (X AND 7)
470 IF M THEN POKE BY, PEEK (BY) AND (255 -
2 ^ BI): GOTO 240
480 POKE BY, PEEK(BY) or (2 ^ BI):GOTO 240
490 REM ****************************
500 REM *** MOVE SPRITE ONLY ***
510 REM ****************************
520 J = NOT PEEK (JOY) AND 15
530 R = PEEK (197)
```

```
540 IF - (( PEEK (JOY) AND 16) = 0) OR R < >
64 THEN 240
550 IF J AND 1 AND Y > 0 THEN Y = Y - 1
560 IF J AND 2 AND Y < 199 THEN Y = Y + 1
570 IF J AND 4 AND X > 0 THEN X = X - 1
580 IF J AND 8 AND X < 319 THEN X = X + 1
590 HI = INT ((X + 21) / 256)
600 POKE V + 16,HI
610 POKE V,X + 21 - 256 * HI
620 POKE V + 1,Y + 30
630 GOTO 520
640 REM **************
650 REM *** HI-RES ***
660 REM **************
670 PRINT CHR$ (147)
680 POKE 53272, PEEK (53272) OR 8
690 POKE 53265, PEEK (53265) OR 32
700 POKE 251,0: POKE 252,4
710 POKE 253,231: POKE 254,7
720 POKE 51832,1
730 SYS CLEAR
740 RETURN
750 REM ************
760 REM *** TEXT ***
770 REM ************
780 PRINT CHR$ (147)
790 POKE 53272,21
800 POKE 53265,27
810 POKE 198,0
820 RETURN
830 REM *************
840 REM *** LOAD ***
850 REM *************
860 GOSUB 1190
870 IF FL THEN 240
880 POKE 2,1: POKE 51717,15
890 POKE 51773,255: POKE 51775,255
900 SYS SL
```

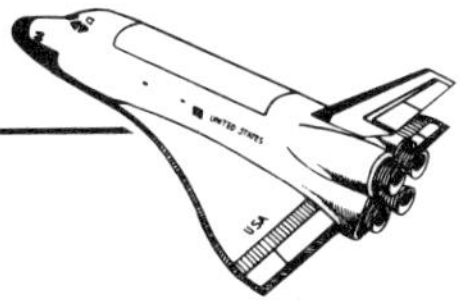

```
910 GOTO 240
920 REM *************
930 REM *** SAVE ***
940 REM *************
950 GOSUB 1190
960 IF FL THEN 240
970 OPEN15,8,15
980 PRINT# 15,"S0:" + NAME$
990 CLOSE15
1000 POKE 2,0: POKE 51717,15
1030 SYS SL
1040 GOTO 240
1050 REM ***************
1060 REM *** MERGE ***
1070 REM ***************
1080 GOSUB 1190
1090 IF FL THEN 240
1100 POKE 2,1
1110 POKE 51717,0
1120 POKE 51773,0: POKE 51775,64
1130 SYS SL
1140 SYSMERG
1150 GOTO 240
1160 REM ******************
1170 REM *** GET NAME ***
1180 REM ******************
1190 POKE V + 21,0: GOSUB 780
1200 NAME$ = "": PRINT
1210 INPUT "PICTURE NAME:";NAME$
1220 IF NAME$ = "" THEN 1330
1230 NAME$ = NAME$ + ".PIC"
1240 L = LEN (NAME$)
1250 IF L > 16 THEN 1190
1260 GOSUB 670
1270 POKE 51753,L
1280 FOR T = 1 TO L
1290 POKE 51753 + T, ASC ( MID$ (NAME$,T,1))
1300 NEXT
```

```
1310 FL = 0: POKE V + 21,1
1320 RETURN
1330 FL = 1: POKE V + 21,1
1340 GOSUB 670
1350 RETURN
1360 REM *******************
1370 REM *** SAVE/LOAD ***
1380 REM *******************
1390 DATA 169,15,162,8,160,15,32,186
1400 DATA 255,173,41,202,162,42,160
1410 DATA 202,32,189,255,165,2,208,35
1420 DATA 169,0,133,251,169,32,133,252
1430 DATA 169,251,162,64,160,63,32,216
1440 DATA 255,96,0,0,0,0,0,0,0,0,0,0
1450 DATA 0,0,0,0,0,0,169,0,162,0,160
1460 DATA 96,32,213,255,96
1470 REM *******************
1480 REM *** MERGE PIC ***
1490 REM *******************
1500 DATA 169,0,133,251,169,32,133,252
1510 DATA 169,0,133,253,169,64,133,254
1520 DATA 160,0,177,253,17,251,145,251
1530 DATA 230,251,208,2,230,252,230,253
1540 DATA 208,2,230,254,165,254,201,95
1550 DATA 144,232,165,253,201,64,144
1560 DATA 226,96
1570 REM ************************
1580 REM *** MEMORY CLEAR***
1590 REM ************************
1600 DATA 160,0,169,0,145,251,166,252
1610 DATA 228,254,144,7,166,251,228
1620 DATA 253,144,1,96,230,251,208,237
1630 DATA 230,252,208,233
1640 REM **************
1650 REM *** SPRITE ***
1660 REM **************
1670 DATA 0,0,4
1680 DATA 0,0,14
```

```
1690 DATA 0,0,31
1700 DATA 0,0,46
1710 DATA 0,0,68
1720 DATA 0,0,168
1730 DATA 0,1,16
1740 DATA 0,2,32
1750 DATA 0,4,64
1760 DATA 0,8,128
1770 DATA 0,17,0
1780 DATA 0,34,0
1790 DATA 0,68,0
1800 DATA 0,136,0
1810 DATA 1,16,0
1820 DATA 2,32,0
1830 DATA 4,64,0
1840 DATA 10,128,0
1850 DATA 17,0,0
1860 DATA 18,0,0
1870 DATA 28,0,0
```

Adventure Character Creator

Many people who like computer programming also play fantasy and adventure games. I enjoy adventure games, so I wanted to design something on the computer that would make character generation less tedious. I like making characters, but let's face it, it takes a lot of time to make a good one. In the main menu of this program, you can:

<D>ESIGN/EDIT A PLAYER
<P>RINT A PLAYER
<R>EAD A CHARACTER FILE
<W>RITE A CHARACTER FILE
<Q>UIT

The command D is the main command of the entire program, so we'll explain that one first. Upon pressing D, you will be put in the second menu of the program. It looks like this:

EDIT/CREATE WHICH:
<1> SCORES
<2> PERSONAL
<3> ARMOR/WEAPONS
<4> EQUIPMENT

Let's enter a 1 for scores. Now the computer will ask you '<C>OMPUTER OR <I>NPUTTED?'. Entering a C will have the computer roll up your ability scores for you. Entering an I will let you input them yourself. If you entered a C, the computer will then ask you for the minimum score on the die. Since it is simulating a six-sided die, it would be best to enter a number from 1–6. Next, you scores are printed out, and the computer asks you if you like them. Enter a Y or a N accordingly, and depending upon your answer, the computer will either do the score routine again, or return you to the menu. If you have already entered scores, it then asks you if you would merely like to edit them. Now enter a 2 for Personal. The computer will ask you a variety of questions such as the following:

<1> PLAYER NAME
<2> CHAR. NAME
<3> CLASS
<4> RACE
<5> ALIGNMENT
<6> ARMOR CLASS
<7> LEVEL
<8> HIT POINTS
<9> MONEY

Remember that you entries for numbers 3–5 must be in lower case, as the computer will check your entries to see if they are valid. The last two options on the second menu allow you to enter your character's equipment, (his armor, weapons, and miscellaneous items). Next, enter a 3, to enter your character's armor and weapons.

Now the computer will list any armor and/or weapons that you have entered. If your list is too long, or if you didn't get a good look, enter an L for LIST. When the computer is finished listing your equipment, it will give you a certain number of commands. The command line looks something like this:

WHICH (A,D,E,I,L):

It is asking you if you would like to Add to the list, Delete from the list, Edit an item, Insert an item, or re-List all of the entries. Entering a carriage return will put you back into the second menu. Each item is given a reference number for deleting, editing, and inserting. Now, return to the master menu. By now, you'll probably want a printout of your character. Enter a 2, and the computer will ask you to line up your printer and press a key. After you do this, your character will be printed out to the printer in an attractive format.

Now that your character has been designed, you can save him on disk, by typing a W. After this is done, you may read him back into memory by typing an R. Remember, when entering a file name, it must be less than 15 characters in length (because the program puts a '&&' at the beginning of all character files). To exit the program, enter a Q.

```
10 CLS$ = CHR$ (147):HOM$ = CHR$(19)
20 PRINT CLS$ CHR$ (144) CHR$(14) CHR$ (8)
30 POKE 53280,1: POKE 53281,1
40 DIM METAL$(14), EQUIP$(29)
50 RVS$ = CHR$ (18):OFF$ = CHR$ (146)
60 FOR T = 0 TO 5
70 READ ABIL$(T)
80 NEXT
90 FOR T = 0 TU 6
100 READ RACE$(T)
110 NEXT
120 FOR T = 0 TO 9
130 READ CLASS$(T)
140 NEXT
150 FOR T = 0 TO 8
160 READ ALIGN$(T)
170 NEXT
180 REM *****************************
190 REM *** GENERATOR MENU ***
200 REM *****************************
210 GOSUB 2780
```

```
220 PRINT HOM$: PRINT : PRINT
230 PRINT “MENU:”: PRINT
240 PRINT “<D>ESIGN/EDIT A PLAYER”
250 PRINT “<P>RINT A PLAYER”
260 PRINT “<R>EAD A CHARACTER FILE”
270 PRINT “<W>RITE A CHARACTER FILE”
280 PRINT “<Q>UIT”
290 PRINT HOM$: PRINT
300 PRINT : PRINT TAB( 5);RVS$“ ”
310 R$ = “”
320 GET R$: IF R$ = “” THEN 320
330 IF R$ = “D” THEN 420
340 IF R$ = “P” THEN 3200
350 IF R$ = “R” THEN 2160
360 IF R$ = “W” THEN 2420
370 IF R$ = “Q” THEN PRINT CLS$: END
380 GOTO 310
390 REM ********************************
400 REM *** DESIGN A CHARACTER ***
410 REM ********************************
420 GOSUB 2780
430 PRINT HOM$: PRINT : PRINT
440 PRINT “EDIT/CREATE WHICH:”;RVS$;“ ”
450 PRINT : PRINT “<1> SCORES”
460 PRINT “<2> PERSONAL”
470 PRINT “<3> ARMOR/WEAPONS”
480 PRINT “<4> EQUIPMENT”
490 GET R$: IF R$ = “” THEN 490
500 IF R$ = “1” AND ABIL(1) < > 0 THEN 750
510 IF R$ = “1” THEN 560
520 IF R$ = “2” THEN 850
530 IF R$ = “3” THEN TY = 0: GOTO 1330
540 IF R$ = “4” THEN TY = 1: GOTO 1330
550 GOTO 210
560 GOSUB 2780: PRINT HOM$
570 PRINT : PRINT
580 PRINT “<C>OMPUTER OR <I>NPUTTED?”
590 PRINT
```

```
600 GET R$: IF R$ = "" THEN 600
610 IF R$ < > "C" AND R$ < > "I" THEN 420
620 IF R$ = "C" THEN 670
630 FOR T = 0 TO 5
640 PRINT ABIL$(T)":";: INPUT ABIL(T)
650 NEXT
660 GOTO 750
670 INPUT "MINIMUM SCORE ON DIE:";MIN
680 IF MIN < 0 OR MIN > 6 THEN 560
690 IF MIN = 0 THEN 420
700 DD = 7 - MIN
710 FOR T = 0 TO 5
720 GOSUB 2700
730 ABIL(T) = D
740 NEXT
750 GOSUB 2780
760 PRINT : PRINT
770 PRINT RVS$"ABILITIES": PRINT
780 FOR T = 0 TO 5
790 PRINT ABIL$(T)":";ABIL(T): NEXT
800 PRINT
810 PRINT "DO YOU LIKE THEM (Y/N)"
820 GET R$: IF R$ = "" THEN 820
830 IF R$ = "N" THEN 560
840 GOTO 420
850 GOSUB 2780
860 PRINT : PRINT
870 PRINT RVS$"PERSONALS": PRINT
880 PRINT "<1> PLAYER NAME.... "MISC$(0)
890 PRINT "<2> CHAR. NAME...... "MISC$(1)
900 PRINT "<3> CLASS................ "MISC$(2)
910 PRINT "<4> RACE................. "MISC$(3)
920 PRINT "<5> ALIGNMENT........ "MISC$(4)
930 PRINT "<6> ARMUR CLASS ... "AC
940 PRINT "<7> LEVEL ............... "LEVEL
950 PRINT "<8> HIT POINTS.........";HP
960 PRINT "<9> MONEY..............";COIN
970 PRINT : PRINT
```

```
980 PRINT
990 PRINT TAB( 0)"WHICH ONE (1-9)"
1000 R$ = ""
1010 GET R$: IF R$ = "" THEN 1010
1020 R = VAL (R$)
1030 IF R < 0 OR R > 9 THEN 420
1040 IF R = 0 THEN 420
1050 PRINT : INPUT "NEW VALUE:";C$
1060 C = VAL (C$)
1070 IF R = 6 THEN AC = C
1080 IF R = 7 THEN LEVEL = C
1090 IF R = 8 THEN HP = C
1100 IF R = 9 THEN COIN = C
1110 IF R > 5 THEN 850
1120 IF R < 3 THEN MISC$(R - 1) = C$ : GOTO
850
1130 IF R = 3 THEN 1200
1140 IF R = 5 THEN 1250
1150 FOR T = 0 TO 6
1160 IF C$ = RACE$(T) THEN 1190
1170 NEXT
1180 GOTO 850
1190 MISC$(3) = C$: GOTO 850
1200 FOR T = 0 TO 9
1210 IF C$ = CLASS$(T) THEN 1240
1220 NEXT
1230 GOTO 850
1240 MISC$(2) = C$: GOTO 850
1250 FOR T = 0 TO 8
1260 IF C$ = ALIGN$(T) THEN 1290
1270 NEXT
1280 GOTO 850
1290 MISC$(4) = C$: GOTO 850
1300 REM ****************************
1310 REM *** ARMOR/WEAPONS ***
1320 REM ****************************
1330 GOSUB 2780:NUM = 15
1340 IF TY = 1 THEN NUM = 30
```

```
1350 PRINT : PRINT
1360 IF TY = 1 THEN PRINT RVS$"EQUIPMENT": GOTO 1380
1370 PRINT RVS$"ARMOR/WEAPONS"
1380 PRINT
1390 IF M(TY) = 0 THEN PRINT RVS$"NONE": GOTO 1450
1400 FOR T = 0 TO M(TY) - 1
1410 PRINT T + 1;":";
1420 IF TY = 0 THEN PRINT METAL$(T); GOTO 1440
1430 PRINT EQUIP$(T)
1440 NEXT
1450 PRINT : PRINT "WHICH (A,D,E,I,L):"
1460 GET R$: IF R$ = "" THEN 1460
1470 IF R$ = "A" AND M(TY) < NUM THEN 1560
1480 IF R$ = "D" THEN 1670
1490 IF R$ = "E" THEN 1800
1500 IF R$ = "I" AND M(TY) < NUM THEN 1970
1510 IF R$ = "L" THEN 1330
1520 GOTO 420
1530 REM ************
1540 REM *** ADD ***
1550 REM ************
1560 C$ = ""
1570 PRINT
1580 PRINT "ITEM#";M(TY) + 1;"=";
1590 INPUT C$
1600 IF C$ = "" THEN 1330
1610 IF TY = 0 THEN METAL$(M(TY)) = C$ : GOTO 1630
1620 EQUIP$(M(TY)) = C$
1630 M(TY) = M(TY) + 1: GOTO 1330
1640 REM ***************
1650 REM *** DELETE ***
1660 REM ***************
1670 C$ = ""
1680 PRINT
```

```
1690 INPUT "ITEM# TO DELETE:";C$
1700 IF C = " " THEN 1330
1710 C = VAL (C$) - 1
1720 IF C < 0 OR C > M(TY) - THEN 1330
1730 FOR T = C TO M(TY) - 2
1740 IF TY = 0 THEN METAL$(T) = METAL$(T
+ 1)
1750 IF TY = 1 THEN EQUIP$(T) = EQUIP$(T
+ 1)
1760 NEXT :M(TY) = M(TY) - 1: GOTO 1330
1770 REM ************
1780 REM *** EDIT ***
1790 REM ************
1800 C$ = ""
1810 PRINT : INPUT "ITEM# TO EDIT:";C$
1820 IF C$ = "" THEN 1330
1830 C = VAL (C$) - 1
1840 IF C < 0 OR C > M(TY) - 1 THEN 1330
1850 PRINT : PRINT C + 1;":";
1860 IF TY = 0 THEN PRINT METAL$(C)
1870 IF TY = 1 THEN PRINT EQUIP$(C)
1880 C$ = ""
1890 PRINT : PRINT "ITEM#";C + 1;"=";
1900 INPUT C$
1910 IF C$ = "" THEN 1330
1920 IF TY = 0 THEN METAL$(C) = C$:
GOTO 1330
1930 EQUIP$(C) = C$: GOTO 1330
1940 REM ***************
1950 REM *** INSERT ***
1960 REM ***************
1970 C$ = ""
1980 PRINT
1990 INPUT "ITEM# TO INSERT AT:";C$
2000 IF C$ = "" THEN 1330
2010 C = VAL (C$) - 1
2020 IF C < 0 OR C > M(TY) - 1 THEN 1330
2030 C$ = ""
```

```
2040 PRINT : PRINT "ITEM#";C + 1;":";
2050 INPUT C$
2060 IF C$ = "" THEN 1330
2070 FOR T = M(TY) TO C + 1 STEP - 1
2080 IF TY = 0 THEN METAL$(T) = METAL$(T
- 1)
2090 IF TY = 1 THEN EQUIP$(T) = EQUIP$(T
- 1)
2100 NEXT : IF TY = 0 THEN METAL$(C) = C$
2110 IF TY = 1 THEN EQUIP$(C) = C$
2120 M(TY) = M(TY) + 1: GOTO 1330
2130 REM  ******************************
2140 REM  *** READ A CHARACTER ***
2150 REM  ******************************
2160 GOSUB 2830
2170 IF FILE$ = "" THEN 210
2180 OPEN3,8,3,"0:" + FILE$ + ",S,R"
2190 FOR T = 0 TO 4
2200 INPUT#3,MISC$(T)
2210 NEXT
2220 INPUT#3,AC
2230 INPUT#3, LEVEL
2240 INPUT#3,HP
2250 INPUT#3,COIN
2260 FOR T = 0 TO 5
2270 INPUT#3,ABIL(T)
2280 NEXT
2290 M(0) = 0
2300 INPUT#3,C$
2310 IF C$ = "END" THEN 2340
2320 METAL$(M(0)) = C$:M(0) = M(0) + 1
2330 GOTO 2300
2340 M(1) = 0
2350 INPUT#3,C$
2360 IF C$ = "END" THEN CLOSE3: GOTO 210
2370 EQUIP$(M(1)) = C$:M(1) = M(1) + 1
2380 GOTO 2350
```

```
2390 REM ******************************
2400 REM ***WRITE A CHARACTER ***
2410 REM ******************************
2420 GOSUB 2830
2430 IF FILE$ = "" THEN 210
2440 OPEN15,8,15
2450 PRINT#15,"S0:";FILE$
2460 CLOSE15
2470 OPEN3,8,3,"0:" + FILE$ + ",S,W"
2480 FOR T = 0 TO 4
2490 PRINT#3,MISC$(T)
2500 NEXT
2510 PRINT#3,AC
2520 PRINT#3,LEVEL
2530 PRINT#3,HP
2540 PRINT#3,COIN
2550 FOR T = 0 TO 5
2560 PRINT#3,ABIL(T)
2570 NEXT
2580 FOR T = 0 TO M(0) - 1
2590 PRINT#3,METAL$(T)
2600 NEXT
2610 PRINT#3,"END"
2620 FOR T= 0 TO M(1) - 1
2630 PRINT#3,EQUIP$(T)
2640 NEXT
2650 PRINT#3,"END"
2660 CLOSE3: GOTO 210
2670 REM ************************
2680 REM *** ROLL THAT DIE! ***
2690 REM ************************
2700 D = 0
2710 FOR A = 1 TO 3
2720 D = D + INT ( RND (1) * DD + MIN)
2730 NEXT
2740 RETURN
2750 REM ******************************
2760 REM *** PRINT TOP BORDER ***
2770 REM ******************************
```

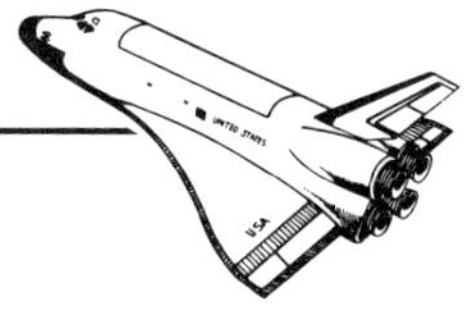

```
2780 PRINT CLS$RVS$ TAB(10)"CHARACTER
GENERATOR"
2790 RETURN
2800 REM ************************
2810 REM *** GET FILE NAME ***
2820 REM ************************
2830 GOSUB 2780:FILE$ = ""
2850 PRINT : PRINT
2860 PRINT "FILE NAME:";
2870 INPUT FILE$
2880 IF FILE$ = "" THEN 2910
2890 IF LEN (FILE$) < 2 OR LEN (FILE$) > 14
THEN 2830
2900 FILE$ = "&&" + FILE$
2910 RETURN
2920 REM *****************
2930 REM *** ABILITIES ***
2940 REM *****************
2950 DATA STRENGTH,INTELLIGENCE,WISDOM
2960 DATA CONSTITUTION,DEXTERITY
2970 DATA CHARISMA
2980 REM **************
2990 REM **  RACES  **
3000 REM **************
3010 DATA HUMAN,DWARF,GNOME,HALF-ORC
3020 DATA ELF,HALF-ELF,HALFLING
3030 REM *****************
3040 REM *** CLASSES ***
3050 REM *****************
3060 DATA FIGHTER,PALADIN,RANGER
3070 DATA MAGIC-USER,ILLUSIONIST,CLERIC
3080 DATA DRUID,THIEF,ASSASSIN,MONK
3090 REM *********************
3100 REM *** ALIGNMENTS ***
3110 REM *********************
3120 DATA LAWFUL GOOD,CHAOTIC GOOD
3130 DATA NEUTRAL GOOD,LAWFUL NEUTRAL
3140 DATA CHAOTIC NEUTRAL,NEUTRAL
3150 DATA LAWFUL EVIL,CHAOTIC EVIL
```

```
3160 DATA NEUTRAL EVIL
3170 REM **************************
3180 REM *** PRINT A PLAYER ***
3190 REM **************************
3200 PRINT CLS$"ADJUST PRINTER AND PRESS
ANY KEY"
3210 POKE 197,64
3220 IF PEEK (197) = 64 THEN 3220
3240 OPEN1,4,7
3250 CMD1
3260 PRINT : PRINT
3270 PRINT TAB(4)"PLAYER CHARACTER
REFERENCE SHEET"
3280 PRINT : PRINT
3290 PRINT "PERSONAL DATA"
3300 PRINT
3310 PRINT "PLAYER NAME........... "MISC$(0)
3320 PRINT "CHARACTER NAME.... "MISC$(1)
3330 PRINT
3340 PRINT "CLASS ...................... "MISC$(2)
3350 PRINT "RACE ........................ "MISC$(3)
3360 PRINT "ALIGNMENT .............. "MISC$(4)
3370 PRINT "ARMOR CLASS .......... "AC
3380 PRINT "LEVEL ....................... "LEVEL
3390 PRINT "HIT POINTS ................ "HP
3400 PRINT "MONEY ...................... "COIN"GP"
3410 PRINT : PRINT
3420 PRINT "ABILITIES"
3430 PRINT
3440 FOR T = 0 TO 5
3450 PRINT LEFT$ (ABIL$(T) + ". . . . . . . . . .",15)
ABIL(T)
3460 NEXT
3470 PRINT : PRINT
3480 PRINT "EQUIPMENT"
3490 PRINT
3500 FOR T = 0 TO M(0) - 1
3510 PRINT METAL$(T)
```

```
3520 NEXT
3530 FOR T = 0 TO M(1) - 1
3540 PRINT EQUIP$(T)
3550 NEXT
3560 PRINT #1
3570 CLOSE1
3580 REM
3590 GOTO 210
```

Unknown Crypt

To go along with the Adventure Character Creator, I thought about making a labyrinth. After a few unsuccessful attempts, I gave it up as hopeless. At last I settled on a compromise. If I couldn't make a complete labyrinth, why not just make a program to describe a labyrinth? This attempt brought much more success. The Unknown Crypt was born!

The theory behind it is easy. First I put all of the commands into DATA statements, which are read into an array. Every time you enter a command, it is checked against those in the array. If it matches, then it will return to the program. Once back, the program decides how to respond to the entered command. Each different room in the labyrinth is basically a different subroutine. If you type in N for north, then the computer will GOTO the program line which describes the area you are moving into. It is really quite easy to get your own labyrinth started this way. Have fun with it and build onto it, or make your own.

```
10 CLS$=CHR$(147) : HM$=CHR$(19)
20 RVS$=CHR$(18) : OF$=CHR$(146)
30 DIM COM$(12)
40 OPEN 1,0
50 FOR T=0 TO 11
60 READ COM$(T)
70 NEXT
80 PRINT CLS$CHR$(144)CHR$(14)CHR$(8)
90 POKE 53280,1 : POKE 53281,1
100 REM ******************************
110 REM *** START OF LABYRINTH ***
120 REM ******************************
130 GOSUB 860: PRINT
140 PRINT RVS$"ENTRANCE TO PUB"OF$
150 PRINT "YOU ARE SOUTH OF THE ENTRANCE
TO AN OLD DECREPIT PUB. IT HAS LONG";
160 PRINT " BEEN VACANT, NOW ONLY THE
```

```
RATS REMAIN. THE BUILDING,";
170 PRINT "ALTHOUGH NOT PLEASING TO THE
EYE, DOES APPEAR STURDY."
180 GOSUB 620
190 IF S=1 THEN S=0 : GOTO 180
200 IF COM$="N" THEN 270
210 IF COM$="L" THEN 130
220 GOSUB 880
230 GOTO 180
240 REM ************************
250 REM *** FOYER OF PUB ***
260 REM ************************
270 GOSUB 860 : PRINT
280 PRINT RV$"FOYER OF PUB"OF$
290 PRINT "THE INSIDE OF THE PUB REVEALS A
DUSTY, COBWEB-FILLED ROOM.";
300 PRINT " MANY PICNIC-TYPE TABLES ARE
SCATTERED THROUGHOUT. ON ";
310 PRINT " THEM LAY VARIOUS MUGS, STEINS
AND OTHER CONTAINERS. ALL ARE ";
320 PRINT "EMPTY. ALONG THE WEST WALL IS
A BAR, CONTAINING A VARIETY OF ";
330 PRINT "BOTTLES. A MIRROR SPANS THE
LENGTH OF THE BAR AGAINST THE WALL."
340 PRINT "TO THE EAST IS A STAIRCASE
GOING UP, AND TO THE NORTH IS ONE GOING ";
350 PRINT "DOWN. ON THE STAIRCASE YOU
NOTICE A GREEN MOSS UNLIKE ANY YOU'VE ";
360 PRINT "EVER SEEN BEFORE, GROWING ON
THE STAIRS."
370 PRINT "ALONG THE NORTH WALL ON THE
WEST SIDE OF THE ROOM IS A DOOR. ";
380 PRINT "PROBABLY THE EXIT. CENTERED IN
THE ROOM, CLOSE TO THE EAST STAIR";
390 PRINT "WAY, IS A WELL. IT IS CLOSE TO
FOUR FEET IN DIAMETER. ";
400 PRINT "IT CANNOT BE TOLD BY MERELY
LOOKING INTO IT, ITS ";
```

```
410 PRINT "DEPTH."
420 PRINT RVS$"MORE"OF$
430 GET R$ : IF R$<>CHR$(32) THEN 430
440 GOSUB 860 : PRINT
450 PRINT RV$"FOYER OF PUB"OF$
460 PRINT "THERE IS NO TYPE OF PULLEY SYSTEM IN IT ";
470 PRINT " WHATSOEVER, ALTHOUGH IT LOOKS LIKE IT ONCE HAD ONE. YOU NOTICE";
480 PRINT " A DARK SUBSTANCE AROUND THE RIM OF THE WELL."
490 PRINT "THERE IS A FOUL SMELL IN THE ROOM, POSSIBLY COMING . . FROM ";
500 PRINT "WITHIN THE WELL ITSELF."
510 PRINT "TO THE SOUTH IS THE DOOR FROM WHICH YOU ENTERED."
520 GOSUB 620
530 IF S=1 THEN S=0 : GOTO 520
540 IF COM$="S" THEN 130
550 IF COM$="L" THEN 270
560 GOSUB 880
570 GOTO 520
580 REM ********************
590 REM *** COMMANDS ***
600 REM ********************
610 DATA N,S,E,W,NE,NW,SE,SW,U,D,Q,I
620 PRINT
630 PRINT "COMMAND:";
640 INPUT#1,COM$
650 PRINT
660 FOR T=0 TO 11
670 IF COM$<>COM$(T) THEN NEXT : GOTO 800
680 T=20 : NEXT
690 IF COM$="Q" THEN 710
700 RETURN
710 PRINT : S=1
720 PRINT "ARE YOU SURE (Y/N):";
730 INPUT#1,A$
```

```
740 PRINT
750 IF A$="Y" THEN END
760 S=0 : GOTO 620
770 REM ****************************
780 REM *** ILLEGAL COMMAND ***
790 REM ****************************
800 PRINT
810 PRINT "ILLEGAL COMMAND, TRY AGAIN . . ."
820 GOTO 620
830 REM *********************
840 REM *** PRINT TITLE ***
850 REM *********************
860 PRINT CHR$(147)RVS$" LABYRINTH
#1. . . .THE CRYPT OF THE UNKNOWN "
870 RETURN
880 PRINT : PRINT "NOT APPLICABLE HERE"
890 RETURN
```

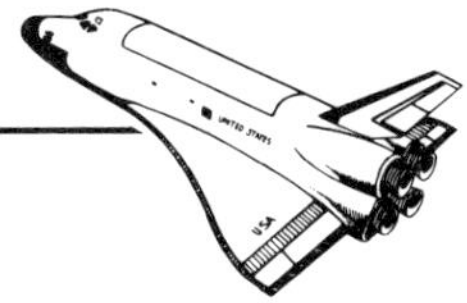

Stereo Graphic

The COMMODORE 64's graphics keys are a wonderful feature that rarely get used to their maximum potential. I decided to make a picture using just graphics characters. Boy, was I surprised! The result is unbelievable. The program prints out a working stereo. When you first RUN the program it will ask you for the time. Enter it in as four digits. For example, if it is 3:45, then enter 0345. This program is strictly for show, but it is fascinating to watch.

```
10 REM ********************
20 REM ***SET SCREEN ***
30 REM ********************
40 PRINT CHR$(147)CHR$(144)
50 POKE 53280,1 : POKE 53281,1
60 A$(0)=CHR$(109)+CHR$(32)+CHR$(32)
70 A$(1)=CHR$(32)+CHR$(98)+CHR$(32)
80 A$(2)=CHR$(32)+CHR$(32)+CHR$(110)
90 REM ********************
100 REM *** INPUT TIME ***
110 REM ********************
120 INPUT "THE TIME IS:";T$
130 IF LEN(T$)<>4 THEN 120
140 IF VAL(T$)<100 OR VAL(T$)>1259
THEN 120
150 TI$=T$+"00"
160 REM ***********************
170 REM *** PRINT STEREO ***
180 REM ***********************
190 PRINT CHR$(147)
200 PRINT : PRINT : PRINT
210 PRINT TAB(8);
220 FOR T=1 TO 25
230 PRINT CHR$(185);
240 NEXT : PRINT
250 PRINT TAB(7) CHR$(206) TAB(30) CHR$(207)
CHR$(208) CHR$(32) CHR$(205)
```

```
260 PRINT TAB(6) CHR$(206) TAB(20) CHR$(213)
CHR$(201)TAB(30);
270 PRINT CHR$(204) CHR$(186) CHR$(184)
CHR$(180) CHR$(205)
280 PRINT TAB(5) CHR$(206) CHR$(32)
CHR$(207);
290 FOR T=1 TO 25
300 PRINT CHR$(183);
310 NEXT
320 PRINT CHR$(208) CHR$(32) CHR$(205)
330 PRINT TAB(4)CHR$(207);
340 FOR T=1 TO 31
350 PRINT CHR$(183);
360 NEXT
370 PRINT CHR$(208)
380 PRINT TAB(4) CHR$(180)
"PANASONIC"TAB(36) CHR$(170)
390 PRINT TAB(4) CHR$(180) CHR$(207);
400 FOR T=1 TO 22
410 PRINT CHR$(183);
420 NEXT
430 PRINT CHR$(208) CHR$(213) CHR$(192)
CHR$(192) CHR$(192) CHR$(192);
440 PRINT CHR$(192) CHR$(201) CHR$(170)
450 PRINT TAB(4) CHR$(180) CHR$(180);
460 FOR T=1 TO 22
470 PRINT CHR$(221);
480 NEXT
490 PRINT CHR$(170) CHR$(221) CHR$(48)
CHR$(48) CHR$(58) CHR$(48);
500 PRINT CHR$(48) CHR$(221) CHR$(170)
510 PRINT TAB(4) CHR$(180) CHR$(180) TAB(28)
CHR$(170) CHR$(202);
520 PRINT CHR$(192) CHR$(192) CHR$(192)
CHR$(192) CHR$(192) CHR$(203) CHR$(170)
530 PRINT TAB(4) CHR$(180) CHR$(204);
540 FOR T=1 TO 22
550 PRINT CHR$(175);
```

```
560 NEXT
570 PRINT CHR$(186) TAB(36) CHR$(170)
580 PRINT TAB(4) CHR$(204);
590 FOR T=1 TO 31
600 PRINT CHR$(175);
610 NEXT
620 PRINT CHR$(186)
630 FOR T=1 TO 4
640 PRINT TAB(4) CHR$(180) TAB(36) CHR$(170)
650 NEXT
660 PRINT TAB(4) CHR$(108);
670 FOR T=1 TO 31
680 PRINT CHR$(175);
690 NEXT
700 PRINT CHR$(186)
710 PRINT CHR$(19)
720 FOR T=1 TO 17
730 PRINT
740 NEXT
750 PRINT TAB(32) CHR$(117) CHR$(99)
CHR$(105)
760 X=6 : BA=1504
770 FOR P=6 TO 27
780 POKE BA+54272+P,0
790 POKE 1664+P+54272,0
800 POKE 1744+P+54272,0
810 NEXT
820 REM  *************************
830 REM  *** MOVE DOO-DADS ***
840 REM  *************************
850 PRINT CHR$(19)
860 POKE BA+X,30
870 GOSUB 990
880 PRINT CHR$(19)
890 FOR T=1 TO 10
900 PRINT : NEXT
910 PRINT TAB(30) LEFT$(TI$,2) ":"MID$(TI$,3,2)
920 A=INT(RND(1)*3-1)
```

```
930 IF A=0 THEN 920
940 POKE BA+X,32
950 X=X+A
960 IF X>27 THEN X=27
970 IF X<7 THEN X=7
980 GOTO 850
990 X1=INT(RND(1)*5+3)
1000 X2=INT(RND(1)*5+3)
1010 FOR T=7 TO X1+7
1020 POKE 1664+T,160
1030 NEXT
1040 FPR T=X1+7 TO 20
1050 POKE 1664+T,32
1060 NEXT
1070 FOR T=7 TO X2+7
1080 POKE 1744+T,160
1090 NEXT
1100 FOR T=X2+7 TO 20
1110 POKE 1744+T,32
1120 NEXT
1130 PRINT CHR$(19)
1140 FOR T=1 TO 16
1150 PRINT
1160 NEXT
1170 PRINT TAB(32);
1180 I=INT(RND(1)*3)
1190 PRINT A$(I)
1200 RETURN
```

Section 4

Business Programs

- Appointment Scheduler
- Business Graph
- Cash Flow
- Interest Rate
- Computer Checkbook
- Inventory Program

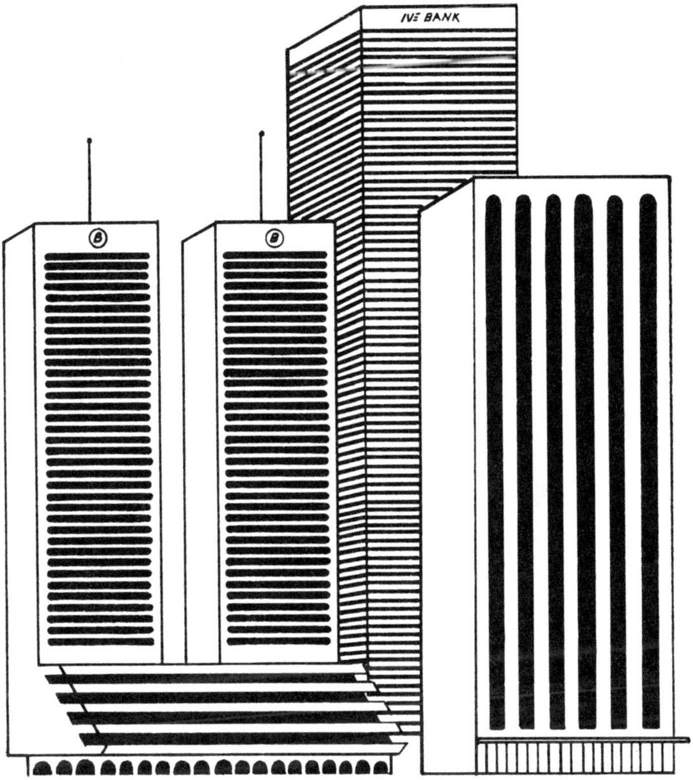

BUSINESS PROGRAMS

Designing a business program for a general audience is somewhat difficult, since many such programs are custom-tailored to a specific company's or person's specifications. What type of program in this category can appeal to a general group of business applications? The programs included in this section can be modified for a specific business need, but most of them are written for *any* business with general business applications.

The five business programs cover a wide range of practical application. The Appointment Scheduler provides the busy business executive with a clear record of the various appointments and other dates on a monthly basis. Business Graph gives a graphic representation of various business trends. This allows the user to see, at a glance, how a business, a stock or any other value changes over a calendar year. Cash Flow shows the *real* value of an investment with a known cash flow over a given number of years. Interest Rate quickly determines how much money can be made with a particular investment over the years, depending on whether it is compounded yearly, quarterly or monthly. The Checkbook program is an accurate and simple way to keep track of what you earn and spend in business, and the Inventory Program will record files of what stock you have, and what stock you have sold. It is a handy database program for the small business person.

The programs can and should be changed to meet your own specific needs. In making such changes, not only can you learn something about programming, but you can also create new ways to evaluate business decisions.

Appointment Scheduler

Business schedules can become hectic if they aren't properly organized, and if an appointment is missed, it can mean the difference between an important contract being gained or lost.

Using Appointment Scheduler, it is easy to keep track of everything from a business meeting to your anniversary. Everything is menu driven. To use it for the first time, you must initialize a file for that month. You do this only once, at the first of the month. (Reinitializing a file will destroy all the data you have saved for that month.) Do this by typing a 5 on the MASTER MENU. Next, it will ask you the month to create a file. Simply enter a three-digit code for the month (e.g., JAN,FEB,MAR). Now you're on your way. The next thing to do is read in your appointments from the disk. Even though there is nothing in the file yet, you still have to do this. It will again ask you for a month, so enter the same month you typed in before. Now you can edit and add dates to the file. Simply enter a 4, and you will be prompted with the following:

<A>dd/<D>elete/<L>ist/<Q>uit:

Enter an A for add. You will be prompted with a date, and a What. Enter the date of your appointment, and hit RETURN, then enter in the date's significance. After doing this, you will see all your appointments listed on the screen, and the previous question re-asked. If at any time you wish to delete an entry, type a D. The program will ask you which entry you wish to delete. Enter the number to the left of the date of your function, and hit RETURN. Your dates will be re-listed, and the number you deleted will no longer be there. Type a Q when you're finished entering in dates. At this point, you can either write the dates to disk, or print them out. First, to be safe, let's write them to disk. Enter a 3, and the month (3 digits), and the computer will do its job. Now that you are back in the MAIN MENU again, you are ready to get a printout of all your appointments. Enter a 1. You will be asked if you wish to direct the output to the <P>rinter or to the <S>creen. Enter a P or an S accordingly. When it's all through listing your appointments, it will ask you to press RETURN. Upon doing so, you will be returned to the MASTER MENU again. Now you're on your own.

Remember, though, to only create a month once, and that before you ever do anything to a month, you must read it in first!

```
10 REM ********************
20 REM *** SET SCREEN ***
30 REM ********************
40 PRINT CHR$(147)CHR$(144)
50 POKE 53280,1 : POKE 53281,1
60 C$=CHR$(13)
70 DIM DAT$(31),WHAT$(31)
80 OPEN 3,0
90 REM **********************
100 REM *** PRINT SCREEN ***
110 REM **********************
120 PRINT CHR$(147)TAB(15)"DATE BOOK"
130 PRINT : PRINT : PRINT
140 PRINT "MENU:" : PRINT
```

```
150 PRINT "<1> PRINT OUT DATES"
160 PRINT "<2> READ IN DATES"
170 PRINT "<3> WRITE OUT DATES"
180 PRINT "<4> EDIT DATES"
190 PRINT "<5> CREATE A MONTH"
200 PRINT "<6> QUIT"
210 PRINT : PRINT "CHOICE:";
220 INPUT#3,A$
230 A= VAL (A$)
240 IF A<1 OR A>6 THEN 220
250 ON A GOTO 300,510,630,770,1220
260 PRINT : PRINT : END
270 REM **********************
280 REM *** PRINT DATES ***
290 REM **********************
300 PRINT CHR$(147)"<P>RINTER OR
<S>CREEN:";
310 INPUT#3,W$
320 IF W$<>"P" AND W$<>"S" THEN 120
330 IF W$="S" THEN 380
340 OPEN 1,4
350 PRINT#1,C$C$
360 PRINT#1,"APPOINTMENTS FOR THE MONTH
OF "MO$
370 PRINT#1,C$
380 PRINT : PRINT
390 FOR T=0 TO CNTR-1
400 IF CNTR=0 THEN PRINT "NONE ENTERED" :
GOTO 430
410 IF W$="P" THEN PRINT#1, DAT$ (T)
C$WHAT$ (T) C$C$
420 PRINT DAT$(T) : PRINT WHAT$(T) : PRINT
430 NEXT
440 PRINT : PRINT "PRESS RETURN WHEN DONE
VIEWING";
450 GET A$ : IF A$<>CHR$(13) THEN 450
460 IF W$="P" THEN CLOSE 1
470 GOTO 120
```

```
480 REM ************************
490 REM *** READ IN DATES ***
500 REM ************************
510 PRINT CHR$(147)"FOR THE MONTH OF:";
520 INPUT#3,MO$
530 IF LEN(MO$)<>3 THEN 120
540 OPEN 2,8,2,"0:DATES-"+MO$+",S,R"
550 CNTR=0
560 INPUT#2,DAT$(CNTR),WHAT$(CNTR)
570 IF DAT$(CNTR)="" OR DAT$(CNTR)="EOF"
THEN 590
580 CNTR=CNTR+1 : GOTO 560
590 CLOSE 2 : GOTO 120
600 REM ***************************
610 REM *** WRITE OUT DATES ***
620 REM ***************************
630 PRINT CHR$(147)"FOR THE MONTH OF:";
640 INPUT#3,MO$
650 IF LEN(MO$)<>3 THEN 120
660 OPEN 15,8,15
670 PRINT#15,"S0:DATES-"+MO$
680 CLOSE 15
690 OPEN 2,8,2,"0:DATES-"+MO$+",S,W"
700 FOR T=0 TO CNTR
710 PRINT#2,DAT$ (T) C$WHAT$ (T)
720 NEXT
730 CLOSE 2 : GOTO 120
740 REM ********************
750 REM ***EDIT DATES ***
760 REM ********************
770 PRINT CHR$(147)
780 FOR T=0 TO CNTR-1
790 IF CNTR=0 THEN PRINT "NONE ENTERED" :
GOTO 830
800 PRINT T+1"-DATE:";DAT$(T)
810 PRINT TAB(4)"WHAT:";WHAT$(T)
820 PRINT
830 NEXT
```

```
840 PRINT : PRINT
"<A>DD/<D>ELETE/<L>IST/<Q>UIT:";
850 INPUT #3,A$
860 PRINT : PRINT
870 IF A$="Q" THEN 120
880 IF A$="L" THEN 770
890 IF A$="D" THEN 1100
900 REM ******************
910 REM *** ADD DATE ***
920 REM ******************
930 IF CNTR>=31 THEN 770
940 PRINT "DATE:";
950 INPUT#3,D$
960 IF D$="Q" THEN 120
970 PRINT
980 PRINT "WHAT:";
990 INPUT#3,W$
1000 IF W$="Q" THEN 120
1010 DAT$(CNTR)=D$
1020 WHAT$(CNTR)=W$
1030 CNTR=CNTR+1
1040 DAT$(CNTR)="EOF"
1050 WHAT$(CNTR)="EOF"
1060 GOTO 770
1070 REM  *********************
1080 REM  *** DELETE DATE ***
1090 REM  *********************
1100 PRINT "ITEM# TO DELETE:";
1110 INPUT#3,NUM
1120 IF NUM<1 OR NUM>CNTR THEN 770
1130 FOR T=NUM-1 TO CNTR-1
1140 DAT$(T)=DAT$(T+1)
1150 WHAT$(T)=WHAT$(T+1)
1160 NEXT
1170 CNTR=CNTR-1
1180 GOTO 770
```

```
1190 REM **************************
1200 REM *** CREATE A MONTH ***
1210 REM **************************
1220 PRINT CHR$(147)"MONTH TO CREATE:";
1230 INPUT#3,MO$
1240 IF LEN(MO$)<>3 THEN 120
1250 OPEN 15,8,15
1260 PRINT#15,"S0:DATES-"+MO$
1270 CLOSE 15
1280 OPEN 2,8,2,"0:DATES-"+MO$+",S,W"
1290 PRINT#2,"EOF"C$"EOF"
1300 CLOSE 2
1310 GOTO 120
```

Business Graph

It's always nice to see profits or losses, buying trends, stock prices and similar business changes in chart or bar graph format. It gives the viewer a much clearer and more useful understanding of the data. That's why the Business Graph program was constructed. It is extremely simple in design, and you can enhance it for your particular business applications. All it asks you for is 12 monthly amounts to graph. Once they have been entered, press a key to view the graph. Each section of the bars is represented by a COMMODORE 64 graphics character. Once the graph is shown, you may press any key to start the program over again. (Remember: BUY LOW, SELL HIGH.)

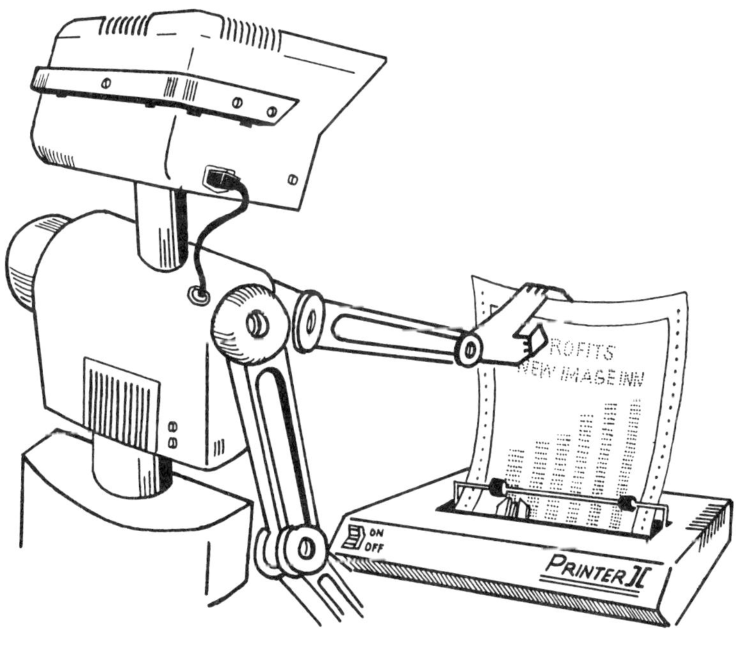

```
10 REM  ***********************
20 REM  *** SET VARIABLES***
30 REM  ***********************
40 M=54272 : AM=40 : F=1.2 : D=98
50 DIM MNTH$(11),MNTH(11)
60 FOR T=0 TO 11
70 READ MNTH$(T)
80 NEXT
90 DATA "JAN","FEB","MAR","APR","MAY"
100 DATA "JUN","JUL","AUG","SEP","OCT"
110 DATA "NOV","DEC"
120 REM  ********************
130 REM  *** SET SCREEN ***
140 REM  ********************
150 PRINT CHR$(147)CHR$(144)CHR$(14)
160 POKE 53280,1 : POKE 53281,1
170 PRINT CHR$(147);
180 PRINT TAB(16)"BAR GRAPH"
190 PRINT : PRINT
200 PRINT "ENTER 12 MONTHLY AMOUNTS"
210 PRINT
220 FOR T=0 TO 11
230 PRINT MNTH$(T)":";
240 DAT$="" : INPUT DAT$
250 MNTH(T)= VAL (DAT$)
260 NEXT
270 PRINT
280 PRINT "PRESS A KEY TO VIEW GRAPH"
290 GET R$ : IF R$="" THEN 290
300 PRINT CHR$(147); : BAS=1027
310 FOR T=0 TO 11
320 IF MNTH(T)<37 THEN NEXT : GOTO 370
330 T=12 : NEXT
340 FOR T=0 TO 11
350 MNTH(T)=MNTH(T)/F
360 NEXT : GOTO 310
370 FOR T=0 TO 11
380 PRINT MNTH$(T)
```

```
390 FOR S=BAS TO BAS+MNTH(T)
400 POKE S,D : POKE S+M,0
410 NEXT
420 BAS=BAS+AM
430 NEXT
440 PRINT
450 PRINT "PRESS ANY KEY TO RUN AGAIN"
460 GET R$ : IF R$="" THEN 460
470 RUN
```

Cash Flow

This type of program is used by many different business people to gain knowledge when deciding on an investment. With a given investment and a known cash flow, the program determines what the rate of inflation would have to be to equal the initial investment. This percentage is evaluated against known rates of inflation to see whether there would be any *real* gain in such an investment. For example, let's say that a company was thinking of investing $100,000 in a project that would have the following cash flow:

Year 1 $50,000
Year 2 $40,000
Year 3 $30,000
Year 4 $20,000
Year 5 $10,000

If the inflation rate were just under 33 percent for each of the five years, the investor would break even. However, since inflation, in the United States at least, is not that high, the *real* return on the initial investment would be pretty good. It does not matter whether the cash flow increases or decreases over the years of the investment, the program will determine what the percent on the investment would be for the period of return.

There is some error built into the program to save execution time. If you wish to increase or decrease what would be an acceptable error, you may do so by changing both the percentage increment and the level of error. It also provides a user entered "starting point" so that you can guess what the rate of inflation would have to be to break even. The program shows you how close you are and then works up or down to find the correct rate. Again, this can be changed to a fixed beginning point if you wish.

```
10 REM *********************
20 REM INPUT INFORMATION
30 REM *********************
40 CLR: PRINT CHR$(147) : PRINT:PRINT
50 INPUT "INITIAL INVESTMENT";PRINCIPAL
60 PRINT:PRINT
70 INPUT "HOW MANY YEARS OF CASH
FLOW";YEARS
80 PRINT:PRINT DIM CF(YEARS): DIM CR(YEARS)
90 FOR X=1 TO YEARS
100 PRINT "CASH FLOW FOR YEAR ";X;
110 INPUT CF(X)
120 NEXT X
130 PRINT : INPUT "EXPECTED RATE";RATE
140 RATE = RATE/100
200 REM ******************
210 REM CALCULATE RATE
220 REM ******************
230 FOR X = 1 TO YEARS
240 CR(X) =(CF(X) - (CF(X) * RATE))
250 SUM = SUM + CR(X)
260 NEXT X
270 REM ERROR LEVEL SET TO $300
280 IF SUM < (PRINCIPAL - 300) THEN 400
290 IF SUM > (PRINCIPAL + 300) THEN 500
300 REM *******************
310 REM THE ACTUAL RATE
320 REM *******************
330 A$= "YOUR ACTUAL RATE IS " : R=RATE *
100: R$= STR$(R); PRINTA$;R$;"%"
340 PRINT "THE ABSOLUTE ERROR IS $";SUM -
PRINCIPAL
350 PRINT:PRINT: PRINT "ANOTHER
CALCULATION (Y/N)";
360 GET A$ : IF A$ = "" THEN 360
370 IF A$ = "Y" THEN 10
380 IF A$ < > "N" THEN 350
390 END
```

```
400 REM **********
410 REM TOO LOW
420 REM **********
430 PRINT RATE * 100;"%","$";SUM
440 IF (PRINCIPAL - SUM) > 1000 THEN RATE
= RATE - .01 : GOTO 460
450 RATE = RATE - .001
460 SUM = 0 : REM RESET THE SUM
470 GOTO 230
500 REM **********
510 REM TOO HIGH
520 REM **********
530 PRINT RATE * 100;"%","$";SUM
540 IF (SUM-PRINCIPAL)> 1000 THEN RATE =
RATE + .01
550 RATE = RATE + .001
560 SUM = 0 : REM RESET THE SUM
570 GOTO 230
```

Interest Rate

When you put money into interest earning programs such as the money market, T-Bills or even a bank account, it's nice to watch your money grow. When interest is compounded with the principal, it can grow at a geometric rate. That's really nice to watch! This little program will show you the growth rate when the initial investment, the interest rate and the period of compounding are known. Entering in the figures, you will quickly be able to see the difference between interest rates and compounding periods. The program is quite simple and you can easily add modifications for your own particular application. (If you are involved in sales, customers like seeing their investments grow too!)

```
10 REM ************************************
20 REM ENTER PRINCIPAL AND INTEREST
30 REM ************************************
40 CLR : PRINT CHR$(147) : PRINT : PRINT
50 INPUT "INITIAL INVESTMENT " ; PRINCIPAL :
PRINT : PRINT
60 INPUT "INTEREST RATE "; RATE : RATE =
RATE/100 : PRINT
70 INPUT "HOW MANY YEARS"; YEARS :PRINT
80 CM$ ="COMPOUNDED AT WHICH
INTERVAL?":L = 20 - LEN(CM$)/2
90 PRINT SPC(L-1); CM$ : PRINT
100 FOR X = 1 TO 3 : READ C$ : PRINT X;". ";C$ :
PRINT : NEXT X
110 PRINT : PRINT "CHOOSE BY NUMBER"
120 GET A$ : IF A$ = " " THEN 120
130 A = VAL(A$)
140 ON A GOSUB 200,300,400
150 DATA YEARLY,QUARTERLY,MONTHLY
160 PRINT : PRINT "AFTER";YEARS;"YEARS, YOU
WILL HAVE $";PRINCIPAL
170 PRINT: INPUT "ANOTHER(Y/N)";AN$
180 IF AN$ = "Y" THEN 10
190 END
200 REM **********************
210 REM YEARLY COMPOUND
220 REM **********************
230 FOR X = 1 TO YEARS
240 SUM = (PRINCIPAL * RATE)
250 PRINCIPAL = PRINCIPAL + SUM
260 NEXT X
270 RETURN
300 REM **************************
310 REM QUARTERLY COMPOUND
320 REM **************************
330 RATE = (RATE/4)
340 FOR X = 1 TO (YEARS * 4)
350 SUM = (PRINCIPAL * RATE)
```

```
360 PRINCIPAL =(PRINCIPAL + SUM)
370 NEXT X
380 RETURN
400 REM ***********************
410 REM MONTHLY COMPOUND
420 REM ***********************
430 RATE = (RATE/12)
440 FOR X = 1 TO (YEARS * 12)
450 SUM = (PRINCIPAL * RATE)
460 PRINCIPAL =(PRINCIPAL + SUM)
470 NEXT X
480 RETURN
```

Computer Checkbook

Balancing a checkbook can be a tedious task, and there is always an element of human error. With a computer, that task becomes more accurate and less time consuming. Enter a 1 to input the starting balance. Then using menu options 2–4, enter in all of your checks, deposits, and adjustments. Press RETURN if you have no more to enter. Then enter a 5 when you would like your ending balance to be calculated. Once this is done, enter a return to re-start the program, or any other key to continue where you left off.

```
10 REM *********************
20 REM *** SET SCREEN***
30 REM *********************
40 PRINT CHR$(147)CHR$(144)
50 POKE 53280,1 : POKE 53281,1
60 DIM CHECK(100),DEP(100),ADJ(50)
70 REM ************************
80 REM *** PRINT SCREEN ***
90 REM ************************
100 PRINT CHR$(147)TAB(15)"CHECKBOOK"
110 PRINT : PRINT
120 PRINT "WHICH:"
130 PRINT
140 PRINT "<1> STARTING BALANCE:"BALANCE
150 PRINT "<2> ENTER CHECKS"
160 PRINT "<3> ENTER DEPOSITS"
170 PRINT "<4> ENTER ADJUSTMENTS"
180 PRINT "<5> CALCULATE ENDING BALANCE"
190 GET R$ : IF R$="" THEN 190
200 R= VAL (R$)
210 IF R<1 OR R>5 THEN 190
220 ON R GOTO 260,320,410,500,590
230 REM **************************
240 REM *** ENTER BALANCE ***
250 REM **************************
260 PRINT CHR$(147)"ENTER BALANCE:";
270 INPUT BALANCE
280 GOTO 100
290 REM ************************
300 REM *** ENTER CHECKS***
310 REM ************************
320 PRINT CHR$(147)
330 PRINT
340 INPUT "CHECK AMOUNT:";CHECK(C)
350 IF CHECK(C)=0 THEN 100
360 C=C+1
370 GOTO 330
```

```
380 REM ***************************
390 REM *** ENTER DEPOSITS ***
400 REM ***************************
410 PRINT CHR$(147)
420 PRINT
430 INPUT "DEPOSIT AMOUNT:";DEP(D)
440 IF DEP(D)=0 THEN 100
450 D=D+1
460 GOTO 420
470 REM *******************************
480 REM *** ENTER ADJUSTMENT ***
490 REM *******************************
500 PRINT CHR$(147)
510 PRINT
520 INPUT "ADJUSTMENT AMOUNT:";ADJ(A)
530 IF ADJ(A)=0 THEN 100
540 A=A+1
550 GOTO 510
560 REM ********************************
570 REM *** CALCULATE BALANCE ***
580 REM ********************************
590 PRINT CHR$(147)"YOUR ENDING BALANCE
IS:";
600 EBAL=BALANCE
610 FOR T=0 TO C
620 EBAL=EBAL-CHECK(T)
630 NEXT
640 FOR T=0 TO D
650 EBAL=EBAL+DEP(T)
660 NEXT
670 FOR T=0 TO A
680 EBAL=EBAL+ADJ(T)
690 NEXT
700 PRINT EBAL
710 PRINT : PRINT
720 PRINT "HIT RETURN TO START OVER, ANY
OTHER TO CONTINUE"
730 GET R$ : IF R$="" THEN 730
```

```
740 IF R$=CHR$(13) THEN RUN
750 GOTO 100
```

Inventory Program

What is a business section without an inventory program? That's exactly what I thought to myself, so here it is. This Inventory Program will store an almost unlimited number of items in a disk file, and the quantities of each in stock. To start up the program, enter a 5 to initialize the inventory file. Enter a Y for "yes" (to initialize the file), and when the computer is done, you are ready to start entering items. Back in the main menu, type a 1 to enter items. The computer will prompt you with ITEM:. Enter the item, for example, "carburetors." Now the computer will ask you for a quantity; enter the number of carburetors you have in stock. After the computer is through storing it to disk, it asks you for another item. If that's all you want to do, then press return. An X appears if you hit RETURN without entering an item, which tells the computer to return to the main menu. Now you are ready to view your entries. Enter a 4, and the computer will ask you if you would like to direct output to the <P>rinter or to the <S>creen. Enter a S, and the computer will display all the entries you have made so far. After a while, your supplies might be depleted, decreased, or all together eliminated. If you wish to update a quantity, then enter 3. You will then be asked which item you wish to update. Enter "carburetors." Now you well be asked for a new quantity. Enter whatever number you wish. When you hit RETURN, the computer will go and update your entry for you, showing you the file's new status. If you would like to delete an entry altogether, then enter a 2. Now enter 'carburetors.' After this is done, your entry will be erased from the file forever. To exit inventory, enter a 6 at the main menu.

```
10 PRINT CHR$ (147) CHR$ (144)
20 POKE 53280,1: POKE 53281,1
30 OPEN1,0:BK$ = CHR$ (157)
40 C$ = CHR$ (13)
50 PRINT CHR$ (147) TAB( 15)"INVENTORY"
60 PRINT : PRINT
70 PRINT "MENU:": PRINT
```

```
80 PRINT "<1> ENTER ITEM"
90 PRINT "<2> DELETE ITEM"
100 PRINT "<3> UPDATE QUANTITY"
110 PRINT "<4> DUMP INVENTORY"
120 PRINT "<5> INITIALIZE FILE"
130 PRINT "<6> QUIT"
140 PRINT CHR$ (19): PRINT : PRINT
150 PRINT TAB( 5);
160 INPUT #1,A$
170 A = VAL (A$)
180 IF A < 1 OR A > 6 THEN 140
190 ON A GOTO 280,520,770,1180,1460
200 REM ************
210 REM *** QUIT ***
220 REM ************
230 PRINT CHR$ (147)"BYE BYE"
240 PRINT : PRINT : END
250 REM ********************
260 REM *** ENTER ITEM ***
270 REM ********************
280 PRINT CHR$ (147) TAB( 14)"ENTER ITEMS"
290 PRINT : PRINT
300 PRINT "ITEM:X"BK$;
310 INPUT#1,ITEM$
320 IF ITEM$ = "X" THEN 50
330 PRINT
340 PRINT "QUANTITY:X"BK$;
350 INPUT #1,QUANT$
360 IF QUANT$ = "X"THEN 50
370 OPEN4,8,4,"0:INVENTORY FILE,S,R"
380 OPEN5,8,5,"0:COPY,S,W"
390 INPUT #4,I$,Q$
400 IF I$ = "EOF" THEN 460
410 PRINT #5,I$C$Q$C$
420 GOTO 390
430 REM ********************
440 REM *** END OF FILE ***
450 REM ********************
```

```
460 PRINT #5,ITEM$C$QUANT$C$
470 GOSUB 1080
480 GOTO 290
490 REM *********************
500 REM *** DELETE ITEM ***
510 REM *********************
520 PRINT CHR$ (147) TAB( 14)"DELETE ITEM"
530 PRINT : PRINT :F = 0
540 PRINT "ENTER ITEM TO DELETE:X"BK$;
550 INPUT #1,ITEM$
560 IF ITEM$ = "X" THEN 50
570 OPEN4,8,4,"0:INVENTORY FILE,S,R"
580 OPEN5,8,5,"0:COPY,S,W"
590 INPUT #4,I$,Q$
600 IF I$ = "EOF" THEN 670
610 IF I$ = ITEM$ THEN QUANT$ = Q$:F =1:
GOTO 590
620 PRINT #5,I$C$Q$
630 GOTO 590
640 REM *********************
650 REM *** END OF FILE ***
660 REM *********************
670 GOSUB 1080
680 PRINT : PRINT
690 IF F = 0 THEN PRINT "ENTRY NOT FOUND!":
GOTO 720
700 PRINT "ITEM:"ITEM$,"QUANTITY:"QUANT$
710 PRINT CHR$ (18)"DELETED"
720 GET R$: IF R$ < > " " THEN 720
730 GOTO 530
740 REM *********************
750 REM *** CHANGE ITEM ***
760 REM *********************
770 PRINT CHR$ (147) TAB( 14)"CHANGE ITEM"
780 PRINT : PRINT
790 PRINT "ITEM TO CHANGE:X"BK$;
800 INPUT #1,ITEM$
810 IF ITEM$ = "X" THEN 50
```

```
820 PRINT : PRINT "NEW QUANTITY:X"BK$;
830 INPUT #1,QUANT$
840 IF QUANT$ = "X" THEN 50
850 OPEN4,8,4,"0:INVENTORY FILE,S,R"
860 OPEN5,8,5"0:COPY,S,W"
870 INPUT #4,I$,Q$
880 IF I$ = "EOF" THEN 1030
890 IF I$ = ITEM$ THEN 950
900 PRINT #5,I$C$Q$
910 GOTO 870
920 REM ************************
930 REM *** ENTRY FOUND***
940 REM ************************
950 PRINT : PRINT
960 PRINT "OLD QUANTITY ON HAND WAS:"Q$
970 PRINT :Q$ = QUANT$
980 PRINT "NEW QUANTITY ON HAND IS:"Q$
990 GOTO 900
1000 REM **********************
1010 REM *** END OF FILE ***
1020 REM **********************
1030 GOSUB 1080
1040 GOTO 50
1050 REM ***********************
1060 REM *** CLOSE FILES ***
1070 REM ***********************
1080 PRINT #5,"EOF"C$"EOF"
1090 CLOSE4:CLOSE5
1100 OPEN 15,8,15
1110 PRINT #15,"S0:INVENTORY FILE"
1120 PRINT #15,"R0:INVENTORY FILE=COPY"
1130 CLOSE15
1140 RETURN
1150 REM *********************
1160 REM *** DUMP FILE ***
1170 REM *********************
1180 PRINT CHR$ (147) TAB( 15)"DUMP FILE"
1190 PRINT : PRINT
```

```
1200 PRINT "TO THE <P>RINTER OR
<S>CREEN:S"BK$;
1210 INPUT #1,O$
1220 IF O$ = "X" THEN 50
1230 IF O$ = "S" THEN 1260
1240 OPEN2,4
1250 PRINT #2,C$, TAB( 10)"INVENTORY FILE"C$
1260 OPEN4,8,4,"0:INVENTORY FILE,S,R"
1270 PRINT CHR$ (147)
1280 INPUT #4,I$,Q$
1290 IF I$ = "EOF" THEN 1390
1300 IF O$ = "S" THEN 1330
1310 PRINT #2,"ITEM:"I$
1320 PRINT #2,"QUANTITY:"Q$C$
1330 PRINT "ITEM:"I$
1340 PRINT "QUANTITY:"Q$C$
1350 GOTO 1280
1360 REM *********************
1370 REM *** END OF FILE ***
1380 REM *********************
1390 CLOSE4:CLOSE2
1400 PRINT : PRINT "END OF FILE"
1410 GET R$: IF R$ < > " " THEN 1410
1420 GOTO 50
1430 REM *************************
1440 REM *** INITIALIZE FILE ***
1450 REM *************************
1460 PRINT CHR$ (147) TAB(12)"INITIALIZE FILE"
1470 PRINT : PRINT
1480 PRINT "ARE YOU SURE(Y/N):N"BK$;
1490 INPUT #1,A$
1500 IF A$ < > "Y" THEN 50
1510 OPEN15,8,15
1520 PRINT #15,"S0:INVENTORY FILE"
1530 CLOSE15
1540 OPEN5,8,5,"0:INVENTORY FILE,S,W"
1550 PRINT #5,"EOF"C$"EOF"
1560 CLOSE5
1570 GOTO 50
```

Section 5

Utility Programs

- Sprite Creator
- Character Designer
- Fast Programmable Characters
- Memory Loader
- Memory Saver
- Memory Clear
- Sequential File Reader
- Disk Menu
- Menu Ideas
- Screen Vortex

UTILITY PROGRAMS

Since this is the utility and programming aids section of the book, I thought it would be a good idea to include some machine language subroutines. I chose machine language for several reasons. First, they are tight and compact. Second, machine language programs are less likely to 'bomb' (malfunction) than are BASIC ones. Another reason, and perhaps the most important, is that machine language programs are far faster in accomplishing a given task than are BASIC programs.

The programs in this section are shown in two formats. The first is the assembled format (this is the 'easy-to-read' version). These types of listings are done with what is called an assembler, a very useful machine language tool. For the programs presented here, I used the **MERLIN** assembler by Southwestern Data Systems. The other format is that of the DATA statements which can be read and POKEd into memory from BASIC. All of these routines can be put into memory anywhere without modification, except for the SAVE and LOAD routines which must be altered. The MERGE routine is particularly useful with the hi-res draw program. Some possible locations of where to put these routines are:

HEX	DEC
\$8000–\$9FFF	32768–40959
\$C000–\$CFFF	49152–53247

These are the hexadecimal ranges and their decimal equivalents. Remember, you use decimal from BASIC!

Let's see an example of how to use one of these subroutines. Here is the BASIC data statement for a fictitious program:

```
DATA 96,60,53,255,32,44,96
```

Let's say we want to start it at location 49152 in memory. Here is how you would use it from a program:

```
10 FOR T=49152 TO 49152+L
20 REM L IS LENGTH OF PROGRAM
30 REM IN OUR CASE, IT'S 7 - COUNT NUMBER
OF DATA STATEMENT
40 READ P
50 POKE T,P
60 NEXT
70 SYS 49152
80 DATA 96,60,53,255,32,44,96
```

That's all there is to it. The SYS command will go and execute the machine language program at the specified address (in our example, location 49152). The programs and subroutines in this section enhance any BASIC or machine language program, and they will make certain programming problems a lot simpler. Also, they represent the first step into more advanced applications.

Sprite Creator

Ah, yes, sprite-making. Is it difficult? No, not really. But it is a problem if you don't know exactly what kind of a shape sprite you want, and you need to experiment. That can take forever, calculating all the bit positions and so on. That my friends, is why you need a sprite-maker. It eliminates the job of thinking out the sprite-making process. Simply move the cross-hairs around on the screen, pressing the space bar when you want a dot, and presto! A SPRITE IS BORN. Your little wonder is constantly shown just below the commands box, (located to the right of the screen). You are given a 24 × 21 box to work with. Move the cross-hair up by typing I, down by typing K, left by typing J, and right by typing L. As pointed out above, press the SPACE BAR to set a dot.

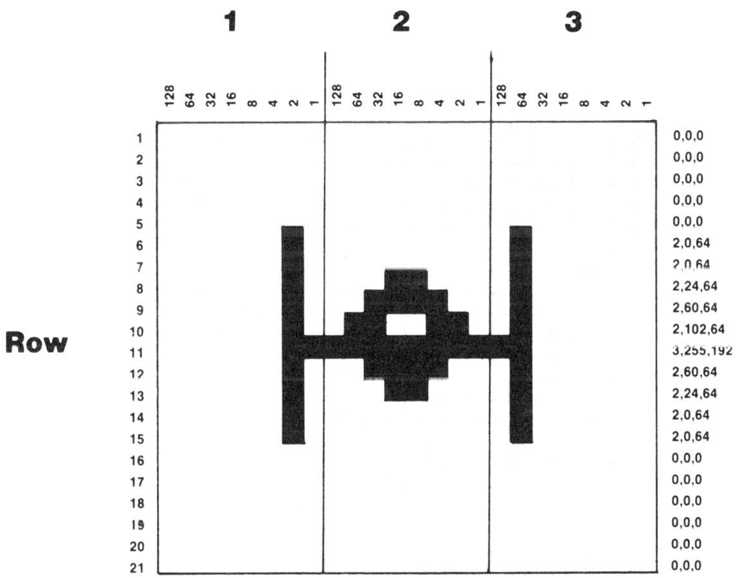

"Sprite Fighter"

The FUNCTION KEYS also perform special functions. F1, when pressed, will display the data statements for the sprite you just created. Pressing F3 once will double the size of the sprite. Press F3 again, and it's size will be cut in half. This will show you how your sprite will look when it is in the expanded mode. F5 clears the screen so that you can create another sprite. *NOTE: When you display the data staments or clear the screen, your sprite in memory will be lost, so make sure you've copied down the sprite's DATA statements before you use either of these options.*

```
10 REM ************************
20 REM *** SET SPRITE UP ***
30 REM ************************
40 V=53248 : POKE 2040,13
50 FOR T=0 TO 63
60 POKE 832+T,0
70 NEXT
80 POKE V+21,1 : POKE V+39,0
90 POKE V,255 : POKE V+23,0
100 POKE V+29,0 : POKE V+1,160
110 REM  ********************
120 REM  *** FIX SCREEN***
130 REM  ********************
140 PRINT CHR$(147)CHR$(144);
150 POKE 53280,1 : POKE 53281,1
160 REM  ***********************
170 REM  *** PRINT SCREEN ***
180 REM  ***********************
190 PRINT TAB(7);
200 PRINT "COMMODORE-64 SPRITE CREATE"
210 PRINT CHR$(19)
220 PRINT TAB(1);
230 FOR T=1 TO 24
240 PRINT CHR$(164);
250 NEXT
260 PRINT
270 FOR T=1 TO 21
```

```
280 PRINT CHR$(167)TAB(25)CHR$(165)
290 NEXT
300 PRINT TAB(1);
310 FOR T=1 TO 24
320 PRINT CHR$(163);
330 NEXT
340 REM ******************************
350 REM *** PRINT COMMANDS ***
360 REM ******************************
370 PRINT CHR$(19)
380 PRINT : PRINT : PRINT
390 RESTORE
400 FOR T=1 TO 9
410 READ T$ : PRINT TAB(26);T$
420 NEXT
430 REM ******************************
440 REM *** INITIALIZE POSITION ***
450 REM ******************************
460 LOC=1105 : X=0: Y=0
470 GOSUB 1040
480 REM *************************
490 REM *** GET KEYPRESS ***
500 REM *************************
510 POKE 197,64 : R= PEEK (197)
520 IF R=64 THEN 510
530 IF SS=1 THEN 550
540 POKE LOC,32
550 IF R=34 THEN LOC=LOC-1:X=X-1
560 IF X=-1 THEN X=23: LOC=LOC+24
570 IF R=42 THEN LOC=LOC+1 : X=X+1
580 IF X=24 THEN X=0 : LOC=LOC-24
590 IF R=37 THEN LOC=LOC+40 : Y=Y+1
600 IF LOC>1928 THEN LOC=1105+X : Y=0
610 IF R=33 THEN LOC=LOC-40 : Y-Y-1
620 IF LOC<1105 THEN LOC=1905+X : Y=20
630 IF R=6 THEN RUN
640 IF R=5 THEN 700
650 IF R=60 THEN 760
```

```
660 IF R=4 THEN 860
670 SS=0 : GOSUB 1040
680 POKE 197,0: POKE 198,0
690 GOTO 510
700 G=1 : IF PEEK (V+29) THEN G=0
710 POKE V+29,G : POKE V+23,G
720 GOTO 680
730 REM ************************************
740 REM *** PUT A DOT ON THE SCREEN ***
750 REM ************************************
760 POKE LOC,81
770 POKE LOC+54272,6
780 POKE 198,0 : SS=1
790 CH=832+ INT (X/8)+3*Y
800 B=7-(X AND 7)
810 POKE CH, PEEK (CH) OR (2^B)
820 GOTO 510
830 REM ****************************
840 REM *** SHOW SPRITE DATA ***
850 REM ****************************
860 POKE 198,0
870 POKE V+21,0
880 PRINT CHR$(147);
890 PRINT "HERE IS THE SPRITE'S DATA"
900 PRINT
910 FOR T=832 TO 892 STEP 3
920 PRINT "DATA";
930 FOR S=T TO T+2
940 PRINT PEEK (S);
950 IF S<>T+2 THEN PRINT ",";
960 NEXT
970 PRINT
980 NEXT
990 GET R$ : IF R$"" THEN 990
1000 RUN
1010 REM **********************************
1020 REM *** CROSS & DOT ON SCREEN ***
1030 REM **********************************
```

```
1040 POKE LOC,91
1050 POKE LOC+54272,0
1060 CH=832+ INT (X/8)+3*Y
1070 B=7-(X AND 7)
1080 POKE CH, PEEK (CH) AND (255-2^B)
1090 RETURN
1100 REM ******************************
1110 REM *** COMMAND STRINGS ***
1120 REM ******************************
1130 DATA I=UP,K=DOWN,J=LEFT,L=RIGHT
1140 DATA SPC=SET PT,,F1=SHOW DATA
1150 DATA F3=SIZE CHNG,F5=CLR SCREEN
```

Character Designer

Although designing programmable characters is easier to do than designing sprites, it is still time consuming. I found it ten times easier to have a character editor. (This one is *extremely* easy to use.) Your work space is an 8 × 8 area. You move a set of cross hairs around on the screen, and use the SPACE BAR to plot dots to represent parts of your character. To control the cross hair, press I for UP, K for DOWN, J for LEFT, L for RIGHT, and the SPACE BAR to plot dots. The FUNCTION KEYS also have particular purposes: pressing F1 shows the character's DATA statements, F3 clears the screen, and F5 shows your character.

```
10 REM **********************
20 REM *** FIX SCREEN ***
30 REM **********************
40 PRINT CHR$(147)CHR$(144)CHR$(142)
50 POKE 53280,1 : POKE 53281,1
60 POKE 52,48 : POKE 56,48 : CLR
70 REM ************************
80 REM *** PRINT SCREEN ***
90 REM ************************
100 PRINT CHR$(19)TAB(12);
110 PRINT "CHARACTER CREATE"
120 PRINT TAB(1);
130 FOR T=1 TO 8
140 PRINT CHR$(164);
150 NEXT
160 PRINT
170 FOR T=1 TO 8
180 PRINT CHR$(167)TAB(9)CHR$(165)
190 NEXT
200 PRINT TAB(1);
210 FOR T=1 TO 8
220 PRINT CHR$(163);
230 NEXT
240 PRINT
250 REM ****************************
260 REM *** PRINT COMMANDS ***
270 REM ****************************
280 PRINT CHR$(19) : PRINT
290 PRINT : PRINT
300 RESTORE
310 FOR T=Ø TO 6
320 READ T$ : PRINT TAB(26);T$
330 NEXT
340 REM *****************************
350 REM *** INITIALIZE POSITION ***
360 REM *****************************
370 LOC=11Ø5 : X=Ø : Y=Ø
380 GOSUB 91Ø
```

```
390 REM ************************
400 REM *** GET KEYPRESS ***
410 REM ************************
420 POKE 197,64 : R= PEEK (197)
430 IF R=64 THEN 420
440 IF SS=1 THEN 460
450 POKE LOC,32
460 IF R=34 THEN LOC=LOC-1 : X=X-1
470 IF X=-1 THEN X=7 : LOC=LOC+8
480 IF R=42 THEN LOC=LOC+1 : X=X+1
490 IF X=8 THEN X=0 : LOC=LOC-8
500 IF R=37 THEN LOC=LOC+40 : Y=Y+1
510 IF LOC>1392 THEN LOC=1105+X : Y=0
520 IF R=33 THEN LOC=LOC-40 : Y=Y-1
530 IF LOC<1105 THEN LOC=1385+X : Y=20
540 IF R=5 THEN 970
550 IF R=60 THEN 640
560 IF R=4 THEN RUN
580 SS=0 : GOSUB 910
590 POKE 197,0 : POKE 198,0
600 GOTO 420
610 REM ************************************
620 REM *** PUT A DOT ON THE SCREEN ***
630 REM ************************************
640 POKE LOC,  160
650 POKE LOC+54272,6
660 POKE 198,0 : SS=1
670 GOTO 420
680 REM *************************
690 REM *** SHOW CHAR DATA ***
700 REM *************************
710 POKE 198,0
720 PRINT CHR$(147)
730 PRINT "HERE IS YOUR CHARACTER"
740 PRINT
750 PRINT "DATA";
760 FOR T=0 TO 3
770 PRINT BYTE(T);
```

```
780 IF T<3 THEN PRINT ",";
790 NEXT
800 PRINT
810 PRINT "DATA";
820 FOR T=4 TO 7
830 PRINT BYTE(T);
840 IF T<7 THEN PRINT ",";
850 NEXT
860 GET R$ : IF R$="" THEN 860
870 RUN
880 REM ******************************
890 REM *** CROSS ON SCREEN ***
900 REM ******************************
910 POKE LOC,91
920 POKE LOC+54272,0
930 RETURN
940 REM ******************************
950 REM *** SHOW CHARACTER ***
960 REM ******************************
970 FOR Y=0 TO 7 : BYTE(Y)=0
980 FOR X=0 TO 7
990 IF PEEK (1105+40*Y+X)<>160 THEN 1010
1000 BYTE(Y)=BYTE(Y)+2^(ABS(7-X))
1010 NEXT
1020 NEXT
1030 FOR Y=0 TO 7
1040 POKE 12288+Y,BYTE(Y) : NEXT
1050 PRINT CHR$(147)
1060 T=( PEEK (53272) AND 240)+12
1070 POKE 53272,T
1080 PRINT CHR$(147)"@"
1090 POKE 198,0
1100 GET R$ : IF R$="" THEN 1100
1110 POKE 53272,21 : POKE 56334,1
1120 GOTO 710
1130 REM ******************************
1140 REM *** COMMAND STRINGS ***
1150 REM ******************************
```

```
1160 DATA I=UP,K=DOWN,J=LEFT,L=RIGHT
1170 DATA SPC=SET PT
1180 DATA F1 =CLR SCREEN,F3=SHOW CHAR
```

Fast Programmable Characters

If you have ever experimented with programmable characters, you know how long it takes to read in the ASCII characters (0-63). A machine language routine does it in a couple of seconds. Try it with the following BASIC program to see how long it takes. Then, using the assembly program below, try it again. (All of the assembly code is presented in DATA statements if you do not have an assembler.) It is equivalent to the following BASIC program:

BASIC

```
10 PRINT CHR$(142) : REM UPPER CASE
20 POKE 52,48 : POKE 56,48
30 POKE 56334, PEEK (56334) AND 254
40 POKE 1, PEEK (1) AND 251
50 FOR I=0 TO 511
60 POKE I+12288, PEEK (I+53248)
70 NEXT
80 POKE 1, PEEK (1) OR 4
90 POKE 56334, PEEK (56334) OR 1
```

ASSEMBLY LANGUAGE

```
****************************************
*                                      *
* PROGRAMMABLE CHARACTER               *
*                                      *
*          SET-UP ROUTINE              *
*                                      *
****************************************

R6510 EQU $1
FRETOP EQU $33 ;DEC=52
MEMSIZ EQU $37 ;DEC=56
FREE1 EQU $FB
FREE2 EQU $FD
```

```
CHRSTART EQU $3000 ;DEC=12288
CHRROM EQU $D000 ;DEC=53248
ENDCHR EQU $D1FF
CIA1 EQU $DC0E ;DEC=56334
CHROUT EQU $FFD2

START LDA #$8E ;DEC=142
JSR CHROUT
LDA #$30 ;DEC=48
STA FRETOP+1
STA MEMSIZ+1
LDA CIA1
AND #$FE ;DEC=254
STA CIA1
LDA R6510
AND #$FB ;DEC=251
STA R6510
LDA#<CHRROM
STA FREE1
LDA #>CHRROM
STA FREE1+1
LDA #<CHRSTART
STA FREE2
LDA #>CHRSTART
STA FREE2+1
LDY #$0
GETCHR LDA (FREE1),Y
STA (FREE2),Y
INC FREE1
BNE A1
INC FREE1+1
AT INC FREE2
BNE A2
INC FREE2+1
A2 LDA FREE1+1
CMP #>ENDCHR
BLT GETCHR
LDA FREE1
```

```
CMP #<ENDCHR
BLT GETCHR
LDA R6510
ORA #$4
STA R6510
LDA CIA1
ORA #$1
STA CIA1
RTS
```

To replicate the machine language program, the following DATA statements are necessary. To POKE them in for equivalent machine code, simply set up a FOR/NEXT loop to POKE in the DATA that is READ.

BASIC DATA STATEMENTS FOR MACHINE CODE

```
DATA 169,142,32,210,255,169,48,133,52
DATA 133,56,173,14,220,41,254,141,14
DATA 220,165,1,41,251,133,1,169,0,133
DATA 251,169,208,133,252,169,0,133,253
DATA 169,48,133,254,160,0,177,251,145
DATA 253,230,251,208,2,230,252,230,253
DATA 208,2,230,254,165,252,201,209,144
DATA 234,165,251,201,255,144,228,165,1
DATA 9,4,133,1,173,14,220,9,1,141,14
DATA 220,96
```

Memory Loader

If you get into any advanced programming on the COMMODORE 64, chances are that you will want to load a machine language routine into memory. You cannot save a portion of memory, nor can you load a routine on disk into a section of memory from BASIC. Machine language, once again, is the only way to go. (Luckily it's easy.) Sure, you can do it the Commodore way, by saying load 'MACHINE ROUTINE',8,1. But that's messy, because it re-runs your program. This routine doesn't do that. It simply loads the section of memory from disk, and returns to your program, right from where you SYSed it. Now that's nice! As the program is shown here, all it will do is load a program into location 16384($4000). To make a routine load into memory from where it was SAVEd, CHANGE BYTE 6 to 15($0F), and BYTES 23 and 25 to 255($FF). to load a program into a different area of memory than where it was saved, change BYTE 6 to a 0, and BYTES 23 and 25 to the low and high bytes of the location in memory you wish to load the routine into. Here are the DATA statements for the load routine, if you wish to use it from BASIC:

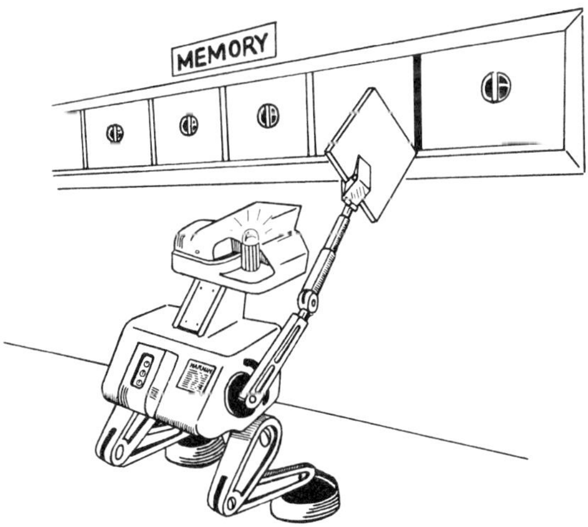

BASIC DATA

```
DATA 169,15,162,8,160,0,32,186,255,173
DATA 37,202,162,38,160,202,32,189,255
DATA 169,0,162,0,160,64,32,213,255,96
```

ASSEMBLY LISTING

```
*******************
*                 *
* MEMORY LOAD *
*                 *
*******************

ORG $CA36

HIRES2 EQU $4000
NAMELEN EQU $CA25
SETLFS EQU $FFBA
SETNAM EQU $FFBD
LOAD EQU $FFD5

START LDA #$F
LDX #$8
LDY #$0
JSR SETLFS
LDANAMELEN
LDX #<NAMELEN+1
LDY #>NAMELEN+1
JSR SETNAM
LDA #$0
LDX #<HIRES2
LDY #>HIRES2
JSR LOAD
RTS
```

Memory Saver

Many times it is useful to be able to save a range of memory to disk. It is difficult from COMMODORE 64 BASIC, so machine language is again the key. As it stands now, this program starts at location 51712 decimal and $CA00 hex. To make it RUN from a different location, some modifications must be made. The program as it is shown now will save a hi-res picture residing at location 8192. To make it save a different range of memory, merely modify the data statements, BYTES 21 & 25 to show the starting address of the SAVE, in low-high byte format, and BYTES 31 & 33 to show the ending address of the SAVE, (again in lo-high byte format).

To give the section of memory you are saving a name, POKE location 51749 with the name's length, and locations 51750–51765 with each ASCII character in the name. An example is given in the Drawing Machine program.

BASIC DATA STATEMENT FOR MACHINE CODE

```
DATA 169,15,162,8,160,15,32,186,255,173
DATA 37,202,162,38,160,202,32,189,255
DATA 169,0,133,251,169,32,133,252,169
DATA 251,162,64,160,63,32,216,255,96,0
DATA 0,0,0,0,0,0,0,0,0,0,0,0,0,0,0,0
```

ASSEMBLY LISTING

```
********************
*                  *
* MEMORY SAVE      *
*                  *
********************

ORG $CA00
```

```
FREE EQU $FB
HIRES EQU $2000
ENDHI EQU $3F40
SETLFS EQU $FFBA
SETNAM EQU $FFBD
SAVE EQU $FFD8

START LDA #15
LDX #8
LDY #15
JSR SETLFS
LDA NAMELEN
LDX #<NAMELEN+1
LDY #>NAMELEN+1
JSR SETNAM
LDA #<HIRES
STA FREE
LDA #>HIRES
STA FREE+1 LDA #FREE
LDX #<ENDHI
LDY #>ENDHI
JSR SAVE RTS
NAMELEN DS 17
```

Memory Clear

When developing the Drawing Machine program for the book, I found that I needed some sort of machine language routine to clear the hi-res screen. Although this routine is not the same as the one in the draw program, it accomplishes the same thing. To use the program from BASIC, just read in and POKE the DATA statements below into memory. As the routine is now, it will clear the hi-res screen. To make it clear another portion of memory, change bytes 2 and 6, to point to the low and high byte of the start of the clear, and bytes 18 and 24 to point to the ending address to which it should clear. Change byte 12 to reflect the character that you wish to store in all of the locations (normally a 0).

BASIC DATA STATEMENTS FOR MACHINE CODE

```
DATA 169,0,133,251,169,32,133,252,160,0
DATA 169,0,145,251,166,252,201,63,144,1
DATA 96,230,251,208,237,230,252,208,233
```

ASSEMBLY LISTING

```
*********************
*                   *
* MEMORY CLEAR*
*                   *
*********************
LOC EQU $FB
HIRES EQU $2000
ENDHI EQU $3F3F

START LDA #<HIRES
STA LOC
LDA #>HIRES
STA LOC+1
LDY #$0
LDA#0
STOREIT STA (LOC),Y
LDX LOC+1
CMP #>ENDHI
BLT INCLOC
LDX LOC
CMP #<ENDHI
BLT INCLOC
RTS
INCLOC INC LOC
BNE STOREIT
INC LOC+1
BNE STOREIT
```

Sequential File Reader

Every once in a while, it seems that I have to check what's in a SEQ file whether it's to verify its contents, or just out of plain curiosity. That's where this program started. Given a file name, File Reader will go through and dump the contents of the file to the screen or to a printer, depending on which you specify at the beginning of the program.

As you become more involved with communications on the COMMODORE 64, you will find that the contents of SEQuential files is very important. This is because most computer-to-computer transmissions use sequential files rather than program files.

```
10 REM *********************
20 REM *** SET SCREEN***
30 REM *********************
40 PRINT CHR$(147)CHR$(144)
50 POKE 53280,1 : POKE 53281,1
60 REM ************************
70 REM *** GET FILENAME ***
80 REM ************************
90 PRINT CHR$(147)"NAME OF FILE TO READ:";
100 FILE$=""
110 INPUT FILE$
120 IF FILE$="" THEN END
130 PRINT : PRINT "<P>RINTER OR <S>CREEN:";
140 INPUT O$
150 IF O$<>"P" AND O$<>"S" THEN END
160 IF O$="S" THEN 190
170 OPEN 1,4
180 CMD 1
190 OPEN 4,8,4,"0:"+FILE$+",S,R"
200 GET#4,A$
210 PRINT A$;
220 IF ST=0 THEN 200
230 IF O$="P" THEN PRINT#1 : CLOSE 1
240 CLOSE 4
250 PRINT : PRINT "END OF FILE"
```

Disk Menu

Sometimes it is convenient to have a program which will show you all of the files on a disk and ask you which one you would like to run. Disk Menu shows you your files, and also has the capability of printing your disk directory to the printer (a handy feature when keeping records). When the program is run, the disk drive will whirr for a few seconds, and then your files will be printed to the screen. If there are more than 17 files on your directory, the computer will print 'PRESS SPC TO CONTINUE THE LISTING' (SPC refers to the SPACE BAR). At this point, press the SPACE BAR to view the other entries, or press any other key to exit. If you press any other key, the cursor will appear in the upper left-hand portion of the screen. It is waiting for input. Enter a 1 to re-list your directory entries. Enter a P to print your files to disk, or if there is a file that you would like executed, then type its number and a carriage RETURN.

```
10 IF FLAG<>1 THEN 40
20 PRINT CHR$(147)"THE MACHINE LANGUAGE PROGRAM IS LOADED"
30 NEW : END
40 PRINT CHR$(147)CHR$(144)
50 POKE 53280,1 : POKE 53281,1
60 DIM FILE$(143),TYP$(143)
70 OPEN 2,0
80 OPEN 15,8,15
90 FOR TYP=0 TO 4
100 READ T$(TYP)
110 NEXT
120 DATA DEL,SEQ,PRG,USR,REL
130 OPEN 5,8,5,"#"
140 BLK=1 : NUM=0 : BYTE=2
150 PRINT#15,"UA:"5;0;18;BLK
160 FOR FILES=1 TO 8
170 PRINT#15,"B-P:"5;BYTE
180 GET#5,T$
190 IF T$="" THEN T$=CHR$(128)
```

```
200 IF T$=CHR$(1) THEN P=9 : NEXT :
GOTO 370
210 TYP$(NUM)=T$(ASC(T$+CHR$(0))-128)
220 GET#5,A$,A$
230 B=""
240 FOR T=0 TO 15
250 GET#5,A$
260 IF A$=CHR$(160) THEN T=17 : GOTO 280
270 B$=B$+A$
280 NEXT
290 FILE$(NUM)=B$
300 BYTE=BYTE+32
310 IF TYP$(NUM)="DEL" THEN 330
320 NUM=NUM+1
330 NEXT FILES
340 BYTE=2
350 BLK=BLK+3
360 GOTO 150
370 NUM=NUM-1
380 CLOSE 15 : CLOSE 5
390 GOSUB 820
400 FOR F=0 TO NUM
410 PRINT TAB(0)RIGHT$(" "+STR$ (F+1),2)
TAB(3)FILE$(F)TAB(20)TYP$(F)
420 IF F=0 THEN 500
430 IF F/17<>INT(F/17) THEN 500
440 GOSUB 780
450 PRINT CHR$(18)"PRESS SPC TO CONTINUE
LISTING";
460 POKE 197,64
470 IF PEEK(197)=64 THEN 470
480 IF PEEK(197)<>60 THEN F=200 : NEXT :
GOTO 520
490 GOSUB 820
500 NEXT
510 GOTO 560
520 GOSUB 780
530 FOR T=1 TO 39
```

```
540 PRINT CHR$(32),
550 NEXT
560 PRINT CHR$(19)
570 POKE 198,0
580 PRINT TAB(8);
590 INPUT#2,PRG$
600 IF LEFT$(PRG$,1)="L" THEN 390
610 IF LEFT$(PRG$,1)="P" THEN 920
620 PRG= VAL (PRG$)
630 IF PRG<1 OR PRG>NUM+1 THEN 560
640 T$(PRG-1)
650 IF T$="DEL" OR T$="REL" OR T$="USR" OR
T$="SEQ" THEN 680
660 CLOSE 2
670 FLAG=1 : LOAD FILE$(PRG-1),8,1
680 GOSUB 780
690 PRINT CHR$(18)"THAT TYPE OF FILE
CANNOT BE RUN";
700 POKE 197,64
710 IF PEEK (197)=64 THEN 710
720 GOSUB 780
730 FOR T=1 TO 39
740 PRINT CHR$(32);
750 NEXT
760 POKE 198,0
770 GOTO 560
780 PRINT CHR$(19)
790 FOR T=1 TO 22
800 PRINT : NEXT
810 RETURN
820 PRINT CHR$(147) CHR$(18) TAB(13) "DISK
COMMANDER"
830 PRINT "PROGRAM:"SPC(7)"NUMBER=RUN"
840 FOR S=1 TO 40
850 PRINT CHR$(101);
860 NEXT
870 PRINT
880 RETURN
```

```
890 REM **************************
900 REM *** PRINT DIRECTORY ***
910 REM **************************
920 PRINT CHR$(147)
930 OPEN 3,4
940 PRINT#3,CHR$(13)
950 PRINT#3,TAB(10)"DISKETTE DIRECTORY"
960 PRINT#3,CHR$(13)
970 FOR T=0 TO NUM
980 PRINT#3,TAB(3)FILE$(T)
990 NEXT
1000 PRINT#3,CHR$(13)
1010 CLOSE 3
1020 GOTO 390
```

Menu Ideas

When developing a program, sooner or later you will usually have to design a menu for it, and an attractive and informative menu could mean the difference between a successful and unsuccessful program. Menu Ideas gives a few ideas on the proper way to make a menu. It uses sprites to help you choose from the four items on the list. Keys A and Z move the sprite up and down next to your list of choices. Pressing the SPACE BAR will choose the item that you are currently next to. Entering an S will toggle back and forth between two different types of sprites. (One is a finger, the other an arrow.) In my opinion, both of them greatly enhance the menu.

```
10 PRINT CHR$(147)
20 CC=0 : BA=1 : BO=1
30 POKE 53280,BO : POKE 53281,BA
40 POKE 646,CC
50 POKE 2040,13 : V=53248
60 POKE V+39,0 : POKE V,63
70 FOR R=0 TO 62
80 READ Q : POKE R+832,Q : NEXT
90 FOR R=0 TO 62
100 READ Q : POKE R+896,Q : NEXT
110 C=0 : POKE V+21,1
120 PRINT CHR$(147)TAB(14)"MENU SELECTOR"
130 PRINT : PRINT : PRINT
140 PRINT TAB(5) CHR$(18) "SPC=SELECT /
A=UP / Z=DOWN / S=SPRITE"
150 PRINT
160 PRINT TAB(8)"CHANGE BACKGROUND
COLOR"
170 PRINT
180 PRINT TAB(8)"CHANGE BACKGROUND
COLOR"
190 PRINT
200 PRINT TAB(8)"CHANGE CHARACTER COLOR"
210 PRINT
```

```
220 PRINT TAB(8)"QUIT"
230 POKE V+1,93+C*16
240 GET R$ : IF R$="" THEN 240
250 IF R$="Z" THEN C=C+1
260 IF R$="A" THEN C=C-1
270 IF R$="S" THEN 460
280 IF C=-1 THEN C=3
290 IF C=4 THEN C=0
300 IF R$=" " THEN 320
310 GOTO 230
320 ON C+1 GOTO 340,380,420
330 PRINT : PRINT : PRINT : END
340 BO=BO+1
350 IF BO=16 THEN BO=0
360 POKE 53280,BO
370 GOTO 240
380 BA=BA+1
390 IF BA=16 THEN BA=0
400 POKE 53281,BA
410 GOTO 240
420 CC=CC+1
430 IF CC=16 THEN CC=0
440 POKE 646,CC
450 GOTO 120
460 X=PEEK(2040)
470 POKE 2040,14
480 IF X=14 THEN POKE 2040,13
490 GOTO 240
500 REM ***********************
510 REM *** FINGER DATA ***
520 REM ***********************
530 DATA 0,0,0
540 DATA 0,0,0
550 DATA 0,0,0
560 DATA 0,0,0
570 DATA 255,255,248
580 DATA 0,0,4
590 DATA 10,128,250
```

```
600 DATA 0,0,133
610 DATA 18,64,133
620 DATA 0,0,137
630 DATA 10,128,242
640 DATA 0,0,4
650 DATA 255,255,248
660 DATA 0,0,0
670 DATA 0,0,0
680 DATA 0,0,0
690 DATA 0,0,0
700 DATA 0,0,0
710 DATA 0,0,0
720 DATA 0,0,0
730 DATA 0,0,0
740 REM **********************
750 REM *** ARROW DATA ***
760 REM **********************
770 DATA 0,1,0
780 DATA 0,1,128
790 DATA 0,1,192
800 DATA 0,1,224
810 DATA 0,1,240
820 DATA 0,1,248
830 DATA 0,1,252
840 DATA 0,1,254
850 DATA 0,1,255
860 DATA 0,1,254
870 DATA 0,1,252
880 DATA 0,1,248
890 DATA 0,1,240
900 DATA 0,1,224
910 DATA 0,1,192
920 DATA 0,1,128
930 DATA 0,1,0
940 DATA 0,0,0
950 DATA 0,0,0
960 DATA 0,0,0
970 DATA 0,0,0
```

Screen Vortex

Screen Vortex is a really neat way of clearing the screen. Using CHR$(147) is fast and efficient, but it doesn't have any style. This little gem will have the screen slowly close in on you. It makes those so-so programs of yours ten times better. . . . or your software back!

```
10 PRINT CHR$(147) CHR$(144)
20 POKE 53280,1 : POKE 53281,1
30 FOR T=49152 TO 49329
40 READ P
50 POKE T,P : NEXT
60 PRINT CHR$(147);
70 FOR T=1 TO 24
80 PRINT "THIS IS JUST A LITTLE SAYING THAT
PRINTS";
90 NEXT
100 SYS 49152
110 GOTO 60
120 DATA 162,39,142,61,3,162,0,142,60,3
130 DATA 169,0,141,62,3,169,4,141,63,3
140 DATA 169,192,141,64,3,169,7,141,65
150 DATA 3,162,24,134,2,169,0,133,251
160 DATA 169,4,133,252,166,2,240,16,24
170 DATA 165,251,105,40,133,251,165,252
180 DATA 105,0,133,252,202,208,240,172
190 DATA 61,3,169,32,145,251,172,60,3
200 DATA 145,251,198,2,16,212,48,2,208
210 DATA 204,160,39,173,62,3,133,253
220 DATA 173,63,3,133,254,169,32,145
230 DATA 253,136,16,251,160,39,173
240 DATA 64,3,133,253,173,65,3,133,254
250 DATA 169,32,145,253,136,16,251,24
260 DATA 169,40,109,62,3,141,62,3,173
270 DATA 63,3,105,0,141,63,3,56,173,64
280 DATA 3,233,40,141,64,3
290 DATA 173,65,3,233,0,141,65,3,160,32
```

```
300 DATA 162,255,202,208,253,136,208
310 DATA 248,238,60,3,206,61,3,173,61,3
320 DATA 201,26,208,159,96
```

Programming Notes